Capitalism and the American Revolution

WE HOLD THESE TRUTHS: AMERICA AT 250

Democracy and the American Revolution

Capitalism and the American Revolution

WE HOLD THESE TRUTHS

AMERICA AT
250

Capitalism and the American Revolution

Edited by Yuval Levin,
Adam J. White, and John Yoo

AEI PRESS

Publisher for the American Enterprise Institute
WASHINGTON, DC

ISBN-13: 978-0-8447-5070-5 (Paperback)

Library of Congress Control Number: 2024952739

This book is the second in a series in AEI's "We Hold These Truths: America at 250" initiative. A full list of published titles appears on the series page.

 PRESS

Publisher for the American Enterprise Institute
for Public Policy Research
1789 Massachusetts Avenue, NW
Washington, DC 20036
www.aei.org

Printed in the United States of America

Contents

Introduction

YUVAL LEVIN

July 4, 2026, will mark the 250th anniversary of the Declaration of Independence and, therefore, of the United States of America. But the year to which that anniversary points us, the revolutionary year of 1776, also saw a kind of birth announcement for another of the modern West's great achievements. In March of that year, the Scottish moral philosopher and proto-economist Adam Smith published *An Inquiry into the Nature and Causes of the Wealth of Nations*. Smith did not invent or launch the market economy, needless to say. But his description of its core assumptions, foundations, and implications stands as a milestone in the history of liberty.

That the United States and what we have come to call capitalism were announced to the world at nearly the same moment is fitting. The United States is now the world's dominant economy by far, and in most respects, it must be counted the wealthiest society in human history. And it is here that the market economy has played the most definitive role in shaping the ethos of a modern nation. The earliest stirrings of what would become the American Revolution also began as a response to some of the abuses of mercantilism—the economic system that modern capitalism arose to critique and replace.

But was the American Revolution—as some of its champions and some of its critics have claimed—fundamentally an economic uprising? Was it a tax revolt motivated by the interests of wealthy merchants and farmers? How were the arguments for representation, democratic accountability, individual liberty, and universal equality espoused by the revolutionaries related to these economic concerns? To what extent were the passions of

1

the broader American public rooted in the sorts of priorities that would come to define our capitalist ethos? And how did our revolutionary roots then give form to the dynamism, energy, and competitive character of America's subsequent economic life? Questions like these are essential to understanding the meaning and heritage of the American Revolution. And it is crucial to ask them not cynically but seriously—in ways not intended to disparage the American revolutionaries' motives and choices but to understand them more fully and therefore also appreciate them more comprehensively.

To better appreciate our country by more fully understanding it is precisely the purpose of the ambitious birthday celebration of which this volume forms a part: The American Enterprise Institute's "We Hold These Truths: America at 250" initiative. Over several years leading up to the anniversary of the Declaration of Independence, we are inviting scholars both within AEI and from other institutions to take up a series of themes important to understanding the American Revolution. These scholars represent various fields and viewpoints, so they will approach these themes from various angles. The papers they produce will be published in a series of edited volumes intended to help Americans think more deeply and clearly about our nation's origins, character, and prospects.

Capitalism and the American Revolution is the second of those books. Its chapters began as papers presented at an AEI conference held in Washington, DC, on April 15, 2024. Other volumes in the series consider the American Revolution in relation to other themes, such as democracy, religion, natural rights, the legacy of slavery, and the Constitution.

The provocation involved in approaching our subject under the heading of "capitalism," rather than "economics" or another more general term, is intentional. We recognize that capitalism began as an epithet and has in some respects become one again. Yet we do not use the term disparagingly. We use it to describe the market economy—its theory and practice, aims and consequences, technical and moral facets, benefits and costs, and ultimately the way of life it describes and to which it is unavoidably attached. To use this term to describe all of that is to self-consciously embrace its champions and critics and seek to learn from both, rather than semantically distance ourselves from one group or the other.

In the chapters that follow, five eminent scholars of economics, history, and public policy consider how we ought to understand modern capitalism and its connection to the American Revolution.

Jay Cost explores the American founders' deep divisions regarding the character of the American economy. The competing collections of views that ultimately cohered around the followers of Thomas Jefferson and Alexander Hamilton had to do with the deep connections between economic and political priorities, and their disputes reached to the core of the early republic's politics and remain relevant in our own day. Cost suggests that the American market economy's development has made it difficult for us to grasp what the Jeffersonians in particular had right—but that recovering a sense of their concerns would be well worth the effort.

Clement Fatovic argues that the American Revolution stemmed from and accelerated powerful trends toward greater social and political equality and that the market character of the American economy had a lot to do with where these trends came from and how they advanced. It was that character of American economic life, he writes, that made the American Revolution not just a repudiation of rule by hereditary elites an ocean away but also a refusal to allow aristocracy to take hold at home.

Deirdre Nansen McCloskey shows that some familiar narratives about the Revolution's economics are misguided. The Americans were not economically downtrodden or oppressed by the British, and the war made America not wealthier but poorer in the near term. The most important implication of the Revolution was the advancement of the fundamental idea of equal liberty—an idea with important economic dimensions, though it was ultimately a moral claim. And its pursuit in practice has been America's great gift to the world.

Richard A. Epstein highlights how the legal and jurisprudential consequences of the Revolution made possible the dramatic economic transformation of American life that ultimately followed. The Revolution as a political matter was a sharp break, he argues, but as a legal matter it involved some crucial continuities. And the combination of the two made for a legal order that prioritized commerce, competition, and a freedom of action that facilitated the miracle of America's subsequent economic growth. But this market-oriented character of American law and constitutionalism has always been controversial and remains intensely contested in our day.

Finally, Christopher DeMuth illustrates how the framework of what he terms "competitive pluralism" characterized the approach of the American founders to economic questions and, ultimately, the deepest kinds of social questions. Drawing on a vast array of examples and evidence, he shows how structured institutional competition has always been key to the distinct character of American public life and that it is evident at the foundation of our economic and political practice. It may harbor the secret to our national success—if we can appreciate its value and continue to apply it.

The range of arguments put forward in these chapters is evidence of the centrality of economic concerns in the thought and action of the American Revolution. But a clear thread nonetheless runs through these varied approaches to the question: Rather than cynically viewing political ideas and movements for change as mere masks for economic interests, we would be wise to understand what we think of as economic concerns as part of a far broader tapestry of interests, forces, and ideas that underlie the public life of a free society. Material and financial concerns don't stand apart from political philosophy or national interest. They are intertwined to an extent that should warn us away from any simpleminded cynicism. No one is purely an economic actor.

Considering the American Revolution through an economic lens is therefore essential but also insufficient. Like this volume, it is just one of several ways to understand the meaning of our founding on this momentous anniversary—and to celebrate its achievement.

1

Capitalism and Republicanism in the Founding Era

JAY COST

It seems as though the left and right can't agree on anything these days—including the American Revolution. Was it a bold stab for universal liberty? Conservatives say of course it was. Was it another effort by a privileged class to exploit the impoverished masses? Progressives, echoing Marxist critiques from a century or more ago, affirm it was. One of the many problems with polarization is that its relentless Manichaeanism prohibits any kind of nuanced thinking. Everything must be all-or-nothing. And so it is with the Revolution—despite that period's incredible subtlety, richness of thought, and fascinating ambiguity.

This is the case with many aspects of the American Revolution, but perhaps none more so than its economic aspect. To what extent was the American Revolution capitalistic? The totalitarian mindset of contemporary debate seemingly requires us to answer that the two were one and the same and then debate whether this was a good thing. But in truth, Americans then had decidedly mixed feelings about what we today would call capitalism. Especially if we expand our time horizon to consider not just the Revolutionary War but the building of a new American state— for the 25-year period between the Revolution and Thomas Jefferson's inauguration—we find an American commitment to capitalism that was equivocal in many respects.

While Americans were nearly unanimous in their support of the rights of private property—holding that the protection of property was one of the central functions of government—they had doubts about many institutions of modern capitalism, or at least contemporary efforts to bring them about. Classical antiquity had taught many of them to be skeptical of wealth inequality, and the Financial and Industrial Revolutions happening in Great Britain likewise inculcated in them a deep mistrust of any political economy that would de-emphasize landownership, which they believed was the great equalizing force in American politics. This group would eventually cohere around the personality of Jefferson, largely in opposition to Alexander Hamilton. An ardent believer in the benevolent effects of economic growth, Hamilton sought to bootstrap the United States into a world power by adopting many of the policies employed in Great Britain.

This divide touched off a heated and sustained political battle, which was resolved only when Jefferson won the presidency in 1800. And while today we take for granted that Hamiltonian economics were superior, we must at the same time acknowledge that the Jeffersonians got the politics more than a little right. Vast inequalities in wealth can and do lead to inequality of political power, which in turn challenges the republican character of our regime. One need not reject the virtues of capitalism to accept that this is one vice. It would behoove us in the 21st century to reconsider this Jeffersonian critique and think through ways we can live in a dynamic capitalist economy that nevertheless treats citizens as truly politically equal.

Liberty and Property

The core principle of modern capitalism is the private ownership of property. As Milton Friedman put it in *Capitalism and Freedom*, the "principles of private property" constitute the bedrock "on which a free enterprise society rests."[1] The founding generation was overwhelmingly disposed to this proposition.

For starters, the modern alternatives to capitalism—socialism and Communism—were wholly impractical, and in the case of Communism not yet invented. The modern administrative state was still a century away, meaning the government simply did not have the capacity to determine the disposition of private property. It would be privately held, by necessity. And in America, those decisions would be widely dispersed. Lacking a hereditary aristocracy and possessing millions of acres of unsettled territory, the future—at least as it was perceptible in the late 18th century—belonged to the yeoman farmer, the man of the preindustrial "middle class."

Moreover, Americans had labored for too long under the contemporaneous alternative to competitive capitalism—mercantilism. The mercantilist system, adopted by the major European empires in the early modern era, posited that colonial systems existed to enrich the mother countries. The British limited the industries Americans could develop so as not to compete with extant manufacturing in the home country. They also restricted the scope of American trade, forbidding American merchants from engaging in direct commerce with foreign powers. The result was widespread discrimination against American property rights that had the cumulative effect of keeping the colonial economy in a state of forced infancy. Americans were free to do with their property as they pleased—so long as they maximized British wealth, which in practice usually meant supplying the home country with natural resources and cash crops to facilitate the latter's Financial and Industrial Revolutions.

The upwardly mobile American colonies chafed under this regime, as it kept them relatively poor to enrich the British. Yet they also had dispassionate and normative reasons to believe in the legitimacy of private property. The politics of the American revolutionary generation, and later those who formed the Constitution, were decidedly Whiggish, inherited from the tradition of British liberalism that grew from the tumult of the 17th century. They agreed with John Locke that not only was private property a right; it was an essential right—the protection of which was at the heart of civil society. Property for Locke was an extension of the person, a product of the mixing of that person's labor with the natural world.

The American Revolution was in many respects an articulation of this Lockean proposition. The famous rallying cry "No taxation without representation" expressed the conviction that there was something almost sacred about an individual's property. The government could not seize it without following established rules. In the Declaration of Independence, Jefferson famously wrote that protecting the rights of "Life, Liberty, and the pursuit of Happiness" was the essential purpose of government. While property goes unmentioned, it is certainly implied. And George Mason, expressing a similar sentiment in the preamble to the Virginia Declaration of Rights, declared that we "enter into a state of society" for "the enjoyment of life and liberty, with the means of acquiring and possessing property, and pursuing and obtaining happiness and safety."[2]

The founding generation was likewise sensitive to the threat unchecked democracy could pose to property rights. If the people at large have the sole power to rule, what is to stop them from seizing the wealth of the propertied few? Hamilton expressed this fear at the Constitutional Convention, arguing that

> in every community where industry is encouraged, there will be a division of it into the few & the many. Hence separate interests will arise. There will be debtors & creditors &c. Give all power to the many, they will oppress the few. Give all power to the few, they will oppress the many. Both therefore ought to have power, that each may defend itself agst. the other.[3]

But he was far from alone. James Madison, in advising Kentucky on how to fashion a new constitution, suggested that property be a qualification for voting rights for the state senate but not the state house:

> To restrain [suffrage] to the landholders will in time exclude too great a proportion of citizens; to extend it to all citizens without regard to property, or even to all who possess a pittance may throw too much power into hands which will either abuse it themselves or sell it to the rich who will abuse it. I have thought it might be a good middle course to narrow this right

in the choice of the least popular, & to enlarge it in that of the more popular branch of the Legislature.[4]

The Constitution and the Bill of Rights are replete with protections of property rights. The federal government cannot seize property without first providing due process, which specifically entails the right to a trial by jury in many instances. Moreover, the taxing authority is specifically intended for the "general Welfare";[5] it was not intended to seize the property of one group to distribute it to another. The contracts clause prohibits the state governments from enacting any law "impairing the Obligation of Contracts."[6] And the design of the Senate had the function of protecting property rights, albeit indirectly. The framers hoped the process of selecting senators—through the state legislators—would elevate men of weight and substance, who would act as a check on the intemperate and more democratic House.

In his defense of the constitutional system in *Federalist* 10, Madison argued that a central purpose of the Constitution was to facilitate the fair resolution of factional disputes, the most dominant being that between those with property and those without:

> The most common and durable source of factions, has been the various and unequal distribution of property. Those who hold, and those who are without property, have ever formed distinct interests in society. Those who are creditors, and those who are debtors, fall under a like discrimination. A landed interest, a manufacturing interest, a mercantile interest, a monied interest, with many lesser interests, grow up of necessity in civilized nations, and divide them into different classes, actuated by different sentiments and views. The regulation of these various and interfering interests forms the principal task of modern legislation, and involves the spirit of party and faction in the necessary and ordinary operations of government.[7]

Madison's idea here is not for an oligarchy, whereby the rich dominate the poor. But it is also not for a democratic tyranny, whereby the unpropertied masses dispossess the wealthy. Instead, Madison envisions the Constitution reconciling these otherwise competing groups around the public good—policies that work for the entire community without denying anybody their rights, including the right to property.

The right to own property is the essential component of modern, competitive capitalism. In this sense, the Revolution, the Constitution, and the course of events in the late 18th century that we commonly take as the "founding" can be said to be capitalistic. Yet capitalism as we understand the concept today entails a large number of ancillary institutions and policies to function—both domestically and internationally. Domestically, access to credit requires financial institutions to provide it and ultimately some central institution to manage the flow of credit. Networks of trade likewise necessitate an expansive merchant class to facilitate capitalist exchanges. Economic diversification implies multiple opportunities for individuals to pursue their talents. Internationally, competitive capitalism requires a mutual commitment to free trade among nations so that capital may flow freely within borders and between them.

On these points, the founding generation often blanched—not always, not universally, and not on every institutional mechanism to support competitive capitalism. But there were important pockets of sustained resistance. Consider, for instance, Hamilton, the first secretary of the Treasury, the architect of the nation's financial system, and in many respects the father of American capitalism. He was a staunch opponent of free trade for the United States. His 1791 *Report on Manufactures* cut against many of Adam Smith's arguments from *The Wealth of Nations* and called for an elaborate protectionist system to facilitate the development of American industry. Hamilton believed the way to maximize American wealth was not open trade with the rest of the world but a careful, programmatic husbanding of essential resources for American use. This, he believed, was a way to overcome "the embarrassments, which have obstructed the progress of our external trade"—namely, colonial America's long suffering under the British mercantile system, which had kept it in an artificial state of economic underdevelopment.[8]

In due course, Hamilton's vision of protectionism would dominate American political economy for over a century, not so much for economic reasons but political ones. Protectionism was of limited (if any) economic value, but it did help policymakers achieve harmony between various economic groups through the application of tariffs. The tariff was of great political use to the Lincolnian Republican Party in stitching together a national political coalition between 1860 and 1932, uniting otherwise disparate factions in New England, the mid-Atlantic, and the West. It was only after the Great Depression—worsened by the extravagantly protective tariff of 1932—that protectionism became widely discredited as a way to achieve national prosperity.

Of course, Hamilton's opposition to free trade was largely instrumental. Hamilton believed in the centrality of private property. He believed in free enterprise. He believed in building out governmental institutions to facilitate the flow of capital. He was, at his core, an 18th-century capitalist. But he saw the United States as a rival of the European powers. The way to grow American wealth was to protect it from foreign meddling. His objections to free trade were thus offered within the broader capitalist conversation.

A much more fundamental critique of competitive capitalism came from those with commitments to classical notions of republicanism. Economically speaking, this republican critique usually stemmed from the agrarian class, which disdained the shift of American wealth away from land into commerce and industry. Politically, it usually came from Jefferson's allies or followers, who organized themselves into the Republican Party in the early 1790s (today remembered anachronistically as the Democratic-Republican Party). Ideologically, their critique had deep roots. The Republicans drew on a tradition stretching back thousands of years, to the golden age of ancient Greece and the last decades of the Roman Republic, that warned about the inequality of wealth, the shift of labor away from yeoman farming, the linkage between money and power, and the threat that an overly acquisitionist ethos could pose to civic virtue. And they pointed specifically to the Financial Revolution that had occurred in Great Britain following the Glorious Revolution of 1688 as modern corollaries to these ancient warnings.

While this faction, which would come to be represented by the Republican Party of Madison and Jefferson, was staunchly committed to private property, it believed that the best type of property for a healthy republic was land and that the government should not facilitate the development of what we today consider modern capitalist institutions, especially banks, which encouraged any number of vices detrimental to good republican government.

Capitalism and Republicanism

The revolutionary American of the late 18th century was simultaneously committed to the principles of liberalism and republicanism. Liberalism was an ideology that emphasized freedom of conscience, due process, and the right to private property. Republicanism was an ideology that envisioned government as the property of the citizenry, responding to the people's direction and working on their behalf alone. Many from the revolutionary generation—men like Robert Morris, Gouverneur Morris (no relation), Rufus King, and above all Hamilton—were convinced that republicanism could be sustained alongside a dynamic commercial economy ultimately supported by the state through institutions like a national bank. Others disagreed, adhering to what historian Lance Banning has called the "Jeffersonian persuasion," so named because Jefferson was the center of political gravity for this faction. Their skepticism toward the modern institutions of competitive capitalism flowed not from a lack of commitment to property rights but rather from an anxiety that these institutions facilitated economic inequality, which challenged the republican principle of political equality among citizens.

The Jeffersonian faction was a sprawling, dynamic force in American politics—encompassing a broad array of ideological commitments, enduring for more than a quarter century, and evolving during that time. That makes it hard to pin down, but a few general points characterize the vast majority of its members. Contra Hamilton, the Jeffersonians generally believed ownership of farmable land was the backbone of a prosperous republic. Landownership promoted a rough (though far from perfect) equality among the citizenry, and it encouraged personal habits like self-sufficiency, personal responsibility, and civic commitment. Their vision for America was an agrarian republic, with the North American continent populated by a sturdy class of yeoman farmers. They worried the transformation of wealth brought about by the Financial Revolution— which was ongoing in Great Britain and which Hamilton sought to begin in the United States—was an existential threat to true republicanism.

The Jeffersonians had a narrative built on philosophy and history that informed their views. No less an eminence than Aristotle believed the ideal body politic was one dominated by the middle class, as it was most likely to avoid the twin disasters of democratic tyranny and oligarchy:

> It is manifest that the best political community is formed by citizens of the middle class . . . for where some possess much, and the others nothing, there may arise an extreme democracy, or a pure oligarchy; or a tyranny may grow out of either extreme. . . . The mean condition of states is clearly best, for no other is free from faction; and where the middle class is large, there are least likely to be factions and dissensions.[9]

At least as significant was the example of the Roman Republic— particularly its collapse into civil war and the emergence of Augustus as its emperor. The classical history of the republic emphasized the class of yeoman farmers as its great strength—independent, virtuous, and willing to serve in its legions during times of war. But after the Roman conquest of Greece, the yeomanry began to decline. After years away from their farms in service to the state, many farmers were forced to sell their land to the wealthy, who imported Greek slaves to work their fields. This growing faction of landless men eventually was consolidated by the warlords of the late republic—Marius, Pompey, and Julius Caesar. By offering them pay, in either plunder or land, these generals turned a large portion of Roman society into their clients, and it was in this way that Caesar was eventually able to overthrow the republic.

The founders also drew important instruction from the experience of northern Italy during the late Middle Ages. Amid consistent conflict between the papacy and the Holy Roman emperor, northern Italian communities like Florence, Genoa, and Milan were able to secure effective independence by the end of the 13th century and reorganized themselves into communes, where power was shared among the citizenry. Yet by the middle of the 16th century, the only republic left in the region was Venice. The rest had been transformed into oligarchies, dominated by the wealthy. Florence proved a harrowing example. Along with Venice, it had held out for decades against the rise of the oligarchs, but the Medici family—grown rich from its extensive banking operations—established a network of clients so influential it could acquire power. And even after the Medicis were overthrown in 1494, their influence throughout the region was still so vast they were able to return to power in 1512. Indeed, the fact that four Renaissance popes were from the Medici clan starkly illustrates the potentially dangerous relationship between economic wealth and governing power.

Ancient Rome and Renaissance Florence provided historical evidence of the theory that economic independence was a prerequisite for political independence. Yeoman farmers who could take care of themselves did not need any patrons to take care of them in exchange for political support. They thus served as a bulwark against the self-aggrandizement of the rich, who are always looking to transform their wealth into power. On the other side, those without means of self-support will gratefully accept patronage, especially in times of economic hardship. This is how a republic, which is a government ruled by and for the citizenry, can be corrupted into an oligarchy, which is a government by and for the benefit of the wealthy.

If Italian history—ancient and modern—demonstrated how disparities in wealth could threaten a republic, the experience of Great Britain in the 18th century identified commercialization and industrialization as twin threats. As a means to fight its wars against France without raising taxes to crippling levels (and thereby entangling Parliament in foreign affairs), the British Crown under William III undertook financial reforms that facilitated what became known as the Financial Revolution. He used revenue from the land tax as a permanent fund to pay interest on the debt. He sanctioned government lotteries. And above all, he chartered the Bank of England, a private-public institution owned by private investors but able to loan money to the government. William's intention was to harness the nation's growing trade wealth for public purposes, and he was successful. William and his successor, Queen Anne, drew on Britain's growing prosperity to check the aspirations of Louis XIV against the Netherlands and Spain.

While Britain's Financial Revolution no doubt created the financial preconditions for its domination over the French, it also brought about substantial, albeit at times subtle, changes in the dynamics of British politics. The combination of growing trade and growing government activity had created a faction of men whose wealth was increasingly in government "paper"—be it the public debt or stock of publicly chartered corporations. Having grown wealthy from public policy, they were not inclined to sit on the sidelines under the assumption that the state would continue to bless them. Instead, they migrated into Parliament, forming a bloc of "purchasable" votes for the Crown.

Not everybody thought this was a bad idea. David Hume, one of the leading figures of the Scottish Enlightenment, thought it was essential to the preservation of the balanced system of king and Parliament:

> The House of Commons stretches not its power, because such
> an usurpation would be contrary to the interest of the majority
> of its members. The crown has so many offices at its disposal,
> that, when assisted by the honest and disinterested part of the

house, it will always command the resolutions of the whole. . . .
We may, therefore, give to this influence what name we please;
we may call it by the invidious appellations of *corruption* and
dependence; but some degree and some kind of it are insepa-
rable from the very nature of the constitution, and necessary
to the preservation of our mixed government.[10] (Emphasis
in original.)

But the losers in this scheme were the landed class, especially its more
prosperous members. For starters, the debt was financed on the back of
a land tax—meaning that it was the landowners effectively subsidizing
the merchants. Their critique was not purely self-interested, however.
They perceived that the Crown had intervened in the people's capacity
to govern through Parliament. Members of the House of Commons, who
were elected by their constituents but followed their own interests at the
behest of royal patronage, were undermining self-government, creating
what economists would today call a principal-agent problem. Elected to
represent their communities, paper wealth had in effect turned them into
agents of the Crown.

Those who stridently denounced this nexus of government and economic power came to be known as the Country Party (as distinguished
from a Court Party, which drew wealth and power from the government
itself). As Cato (the pen name of John Trenchard and Thomas Gordon)
put it,

I would lay it down as a rule for all nations to consider and
observe, that where bribery is practised, 'tis a thousand to one
but mischief is intended; and the more bribery, the more mischief. When therefore the people, or their trustees, are bribed,
they would do well to consider, that it is not, it cannot be, for
their own sakes. Honest and open designs, which will bear light
and examination, are hurt and discredited by base and dark
expedients to bring them about.[11]

Not only did the alliance between the government and this new moneyed class corrupt the representative quality of the British system; it also brought about financial calamity. A speculative bubble surrounding the government-created South Sea Company popped in 1720, leading to widespread economic suffering and proof, in the eyes of the Country Whigs, that the fix was in. As Cato put it,

> To see one's country labouring under all the sad symptoms of distress, without the violence of war, without the diabolical refinements of able politicians; but purely from the dull cunning of inferior rogues, void of bravery, void of abilities; wretches that would run away in the field, and be despised in assemblies; this is what should turn pity into rage, and grief into vengeance.[12]

This was a story the Jeffersonians knew well. They ate up Cato and similar polemicists like Viscount Bolingbroke, both of whom demonstrated to their satisfaction that Great Britain was not a free state but rather the domain of an unduly powerful king and a network of clients grown rich on government paper and royal largesse.

The Jeffersonians were also nonplussed over the prospects of Britain's Industrial Revolution migrating to the Americas. Industrialization had followed on the heels of the Enclosure Movement—as peasants who had been kicked off much of their land were directed into factory work. Great Britain at this point had an extremely limited franchise: One had to be either a landowner or a substantial member of the middle class of merchants and artisans. In America, however, land was plentiful. Why, in the Jeffersonian vision, should Americans give up the farm for life in a factory? They would only sacrifice their economic independence for the whims of what Madison derided as "fashion." In a critique that anticipated future Marxist theory, the Jeffersonians were horrified at the prospect of a nation of small, independent landowners being transformed into wage workers, dependent on the owners of industry and the broader forces of market dynamics. This was no way to maintain a free state.

A consistent theme through these various ideological and historical narratives was that the distribution of political power inevitably mimicked the distribution of economic wealth. Thomas More—an adviser to Henry VIII and leading political theorist of the early modern era—went so far as to envision his theoretical republic, the "Utopia," being built on the common ownership of property. "I'm quite convinced," says More's fictional interlocutor, Raphael,

> that you'll never get a fair distribution of goods, or a satisfactory organization of human life, until you abolish private property altogether. So long as it exists, the vast majority of the human race . . . will inevitably go on labouring under a burden of poverty, hardship, and worry.[13]

The Jeffersonians did not have to resort to such heavy-handed ideas as state control of property. Instead, they believed that the virgin territory of the West would support wave after wave of aspiring yeomen for generations and thus serve as an equalizing force for the new nation. From their perspective, it was madness for the United States to follow in the path of 18th-century Britain. Or if not madness then a deep-seated preference for oligarchy, or even worse, "a monarchy bottomed on corruption."[14] These are the words Jefferson chose to describe Hamilton's ambitions, and it helps explain why the Jeffersonians derided Hamilton—today remembered as the architect of American capitalism—as the great enemy of republicanism.

"One Great American System"

The Jeffersonian persuasion was certainly extant during the revolution, although it remained mostly latent. There was wide agreement among the Americans—be they eventually partial to the ideas of Jefferson or Hamilton—that the colonies had to break free from the yoke of British tyranny. The shared enemy mostly subdued the salience of an eventually significant disagreement. Still, there were portents of the coming divide, mainly thanks to the polarizing figure of Robert Morris.

Morris is a study in contrasts. It is easy to see why those who were suspicious of the Financial Revolution would disdain him, yet at the same time, his contributions to the American Revolution are undeniable; the man still does not get his due. On the one hand, Morris, who made his money as a merchant in Philadelphia, led a life of urban opulence in a nation dominated by yeoman farmers. On the other hand, he staked his own fortune as collateral for American debts. Ultimately, Morris understood that government success depended on institutions that could tap into the nation's commercial wealth, but at the same time—as the premier man of American commerce—he knew it would work to his benefit. So while Morris was the obvious choice to oversee the Continental Congress's finances, he was also an extremely controversial one. Ultimately, anxiety about Morris's vast powers led Congress to redesign how its money was managed, eliminating his old role of superintendent of finance and replacing it with a three-member Board of Treasury.

Washington initially offered the job of secretary of the Treasury to Morris, but the latter turned it down, opting instead to enter the Senate as a member from Pennsylvania. Fatefully, the president then turned to Hamilton, his former aide-de-camp in the Continental Army. Hamilton shared Morris's commitment to a political economy that would stabilize and encourage American capitalism, but he was so much more than this. He was a true visionary—sensing the economic potential of the United States and appreciating how government policy could make that happen. He was also a whirling dervish of activity—a workaholic whose ability to think, write, and advocate was unmatched among his peers. Hamilton being Hamilton, he would be no mere secretary of the Treasury. He instead would become the most divisive and polarizing figure in American politics and, in so doing, would offer enormous clarity around the competing visions of American republicanism.

The beginning of the Hamiltonian era in American political economy can be identified precisely: January 9, 1790, the day his monumental *Report on the Public Credit* was submitted to Congress and unveiled to the nation. This was the first of three reports—followed by the *Report on a National Bank* and the *Report on Manufactures*—that Hamilton would unveil over the next 23 months and in which he would lay out his vision for a commercialized and economically diversified American republic. Hamilton, above and before anybody else, intuited that the Financial and Industrial Revolutions of Great Britain would eventually come to the United States.

Assuming the government instituted the correct policies, the "thirteen States," as Hamilton argued in *Federalist* 11, could erect "one great American system, superior to the controul of all trans-atlantic force or influence, and able to dictate the terms of the connection between the old and the new world!"[15] As secretary of the Treasury, Hamilton prioritized three policies: a permanent, public debt guaranteed by the federal government; a national bank; and government support for manufacturing. Hamilton believed these policies would promote prosperity and, eventually, national unity. Stated simply, if Americans were making money off each other through a robust national economy, they would have more reasons to get along. In *Federalist* 12, he argued that

> the prosperity of commerce is . . . the most useful as well as the most productive source of national wealth; and has accordingly become a primary object of their political cares. . . . It serves to vivify and invigorate the channels of industry, and to make them flow with greater activity and copiousness. The assiduous merchant, the laborious husbandman, the active mechanic, and the industrious manufacturer, all orders of men look forward with eager expectation and growing alacrity to this pleasing reward of their toils. The often-agitated question, between agriculture and commerce, has from indubitable experience received a decision, which has silenced the rivalships, that once subsisted between them, and has proved to the satisfaction of their friends, that their interests are intimately blended and interwoven.[16]

The proper disposition of the public debts was of crucial importance to Hamilton. He wanted a commitment to pay the debts of the country in full—no haircuts for investors. He wanted the debt centralized—shifted away from the states and placed under the aegis of the federal government. These policies would have two important consequences: First, they would make it easier for the United States to borrow money in the future. And second, they would reorient the loyalties of the moneyed class, those who had lent the government cash in the first place, from the states to the federal government. But Hamilton also saw the potential for a funded debt to satisfy one of the preconditions of a capitalist economy: a stable and uniform currency. If people are confident the government will pay back its debts, then a $10 debt certificate will be worth $10 in goods and services, wherever in the country it might be exchanged. Per Hamilton:

> It is a well known fact, that in countries in which the national debt is properly funded, and an object of established confidence, it answers most of the purposes of money. Transfers of stock or public debt are there equivalent to payments in specie; or in other words, stock, in the principal transactions of business, passes current as specie.[17]

Hamilton modeled his Bank of the United States on the Bank of England, a public-private partnership that could lend money to the government in a pinch. Unlike Great Britain, the United States had virtually no banking infrastructure in the 18th century, and literally none outside the major cities of the Atlantic coast. Hamilton intended to place the tax revenues of the federal government in the bank, which then could serve as the initial capital infusion necessary to extend credit to private enterprise:

> Gold and Silver, when they are employed merely as the instruments of exchange and alienation, have been not improperly denominated dead Stock; but when deposited in Banks, to become the basis of a paper circulation, which takes their

character and place, as the signs or representatives of value, they then acquire life, or, in other words, an active and productive quality.[18]

The secretary does not use the phrase "fractional-reserve lending" in his treatise, but he certainly had that concept in mind.

Hamilton's *Report on Manufactures* calls for an elaborate network of government patronage of American industry, which at this point was still in a stage of infancy. As mentioned previously, while Hamilton's program is inconsistent with Smith's arguments for free trade in *The Wealth of Nations*, the divide essentially boils down to an internecine dispute among capitalists. Hamilton agreed with Smith that economic diversification would be key to economic success; he just thought the government should help bootstrap the country to that position.

It is a testament to Hamilton's farsightedness that many of his ideas seem like no-brainers to us today: a national currency with uniform value across the country, a central lending authority to facilitate the proliferation of credit, and a diversified economic base. These were controversial propositions in the late 18th century. Within a few short months of the release of the *Report on Public Credit*, the disparate factions of opponents to his ideas would begin to cohere under the banner of the Republican Party, which Jefferson would helm in due course and which would be committed to the defeat of Hamiltonianism. It is not that Hamilton's opponents despised economic prosperity. Rather, they believed that his vision of an American economy was incompatible with a true republic and more in keeping with an oligarchy. Some suspected that Hamilton's true design was to establish an American monarchy, with himself wielding power from behind the scenes.

The Jeffersonians did not have a problem with a national currency, but they generally believed it should be specie—or precious metals—rather than government paper. After all, using the debt as a national currency would make it a *permanent* debt, one that would therefore give rise to endless opportunities for the moneyed class to profit on government activity and, in so doing, come to control the state itself. This anxiety persisted through a number of Republican writings of the early 1790s, and none more sharply perhaps than Madison's letters to Jefferson. Writing from New York, Madison noted in the summer of 1791 that "stockjobbing drowns every other subject," and that "the gamblers" make an "eternal buzz."[19]

The following month, he warned Jefferson about the growing political power of the bondholders: "The stockjobbers will become the pretorian band of the Government—at once its tool & its tyrant; bribed by its largesses, & overawing it, by clamours & combinations."[20] The reference to the "pretorian band" illustrates how large the example of Rome loomed in the collective imagination of the age. During the imperial age, the military was forbidden from entering the city of Rome, so the emperor was protected by a special group of soldiers known as the Praetorian Guard, but their proximity to the emperor enabled them to murder several emperors and install new ones.. Madison's implication was that Hamilton, having forged such a tight connection with the public bondholders, had effectively handed control of the government to them.

The Bank of the United States was likewise a nonstarter for most Republicans. Jefferson himself articulated some of the sharpest opinions against it, at one point arguing that "banking establishments are more dangerous than standing armies."[21] This was not an idea pulled out of whole cloth, even though it might seem peculiar to modern readers. The Republicans believed the Bank of England was essential to the rise of the moneyed class that had come to dominate British politics in the late Stuart and early Hanoverian eras. And looking back to Renaissance Florence, it was surely no coincidence that the Florentine Republic fell to the Medicis, who had established themselves as Europe's premier banking family, leaving them flush with resources sufficient to purchase loyalty among the citizenry and eventually the Holy See itself.

And the bank could not be seen independently from Hamilton's debt plans, for one could use government debt to purchase two-thirds of bank stock—thereby ensuring that the same people who owned the bank would be the ones who had owned government debt. On the floor of the

House of Representatives, Madison argued that "incorporated societies" had a "great and extensive influence . . . on public affairs in Europe: They are a powerful machine, which have always been found competent to effect objects on principles, in a great measure independent of the people."[22]

Finally, with respect to Hamilton's plan for economic diversification and industrialization, the Republicans likewise were staunchly opposed. Any policy that would so aggressively redirect the country from a commitment to yeoman farmers was unacceptable. In an essay titled "Fashion," Madison made his point by pitying the lamentable state of the British working class:

> An humble address has been lately presented to the Prince of Wales by the BUCKLE MANUFACTURERS of Birmingham, . . . stating that the buckle trade gives employment to more than TWENTY THOUSAND persons, numbers of whom, in consequence of the prevailing fashion of SHOESTRINGS & SLIPPERS, are at present without employ, almost destitute of bread, and exposed to the horrors of want at the most inclement season . . . and finally, IMPLORING his Royal Highness to consider the deplorable condition of their trade, which is in danger of being ruined by the *mutability of fashion*, and to give that direction to the *public taste*, which will insure the lasting gratitude of the petitioners.[23] (Emphasis in original.)

In Madison's judgment, industrial workers are inevitably at the mercy of "mere fashion," for they do not produce the necessities of life. "What a contrast is here," he concluded,

> to the independent situation and manly sentiments of American citizens, who live on their own soil, or whose labour is necessary to its cultivation, or who were occupied in supplying wants, which being founded in solid utility, in comfortable

accommodation, or in settled habits, produce a reciprocity of dependence, at once ensuring subsistence, and inspiring a dignified sense of social rights.[24]

As independent landowners who produce the food necessary to sustain life itself, American citizens do not have to beg the crown prince of Great Britain to change the way he fastens his shoes.

Even though Jefferson became the leader of the Republican faction, Madison was its chief intellectual during its early period. Some of this had to do with where the two men found themselves. Jefferson, being inside Washington's cabinet along with Hamilton, was constrained in what he could do and say. Madison, on the other hand, was in the House, where he took public positions against Hamilton. Madison was also more disposed to polemical writing than Jefferson, having participated (with Hamilton, ironically) in the writing of the Federalist Papers. Many of Madison's most aggressive denunciations of Hamilton's system of finance appeared as anonymous essays for the *National Gazette*, a Republican newspaper that Madison and Jefferson helped found in 1791.

What really comes out in Madison's attacks on Hamilton's system are its political dangers. Emblematic of the Jeffersonian position, Madison is not making an economic case against Hamilton's system. His argument, rather, is that adopting these policies will degrade the republican characteristic of the new nation. Madison was likewise convinced that Hamilton was the head of a faction intent on doing precisely that. In one of his most striking essays, "A Candid State of Parties," he contrasted what he took as the Jeffersonian and Hamilton views of politics:

One of the divisions consists of those, who from particular interest, from natural temper, or from the habits of life, are more partial to the opulent than to the other classes of society. . . . Men of those sentiments must naturally wish to point the measures of government less to the interest of the many than of a few . . . that by giving such a turn to the administration, the government itself may by degrees be narrowed into fewer hands, and approximated to an hereditary form.

The other division consists of those who believing in the doctrine that mankind are capable of governing themselves, and hating hereditary power as an insult to the reason and an outrage to the rights of man, are naturally offended at every public measure that does not appeal to the understanding and to the general interest of the community, or that is not strictly conformable to the principles, and conducive to the preservation of republican government.[25]

Put simply, Madison's objections—and those of the larger Jeffersonian party—to Hamilton's economic policies were substantially political in nature. Hamilton's system would empower the few at the expense of the many and transform the hearty, independent American into a servant of the wealthy and well-connected. Hamilton's vision for a dynamic, commercial, and diversified American economy was, in this view, a vision of oligarchy, if not outright monarchy.

It may seem odd for us today to read Madison denouncing Hamilton for what are essentially core components of our modern capitalist system: a national currency, a centralized bank, and economic diversification. What we must remember is that Madison, like all those of the Jeffersonian persuasion, advanced an ideology that predates the emergence of modern capitalism. Theirs was a critique that went far back into classical antiquity, emphasizing the importance of equal wealth in a republic and looking at the examples of Florence and Great Britain as cautionary tales, in which public policy can distort economic equality and thereby threaten self-government. Their vision was for an "empire of liberty," as Jefferson would later put it, built on the backbone of a network of yeoman farmers stretching across the continent.

Money and Power

The Jeffersonian critique of Hamiltonian economics proved exceptionally durable in American politics. After the War of 1812, a large portion of the Republican coalition—Madison chief among them—reconciled themselves to much of Hamilton's system, including a national bank. They recognized that commercial vigor and economic diversification were necessary to secure American prestige and independence, just as Hamilton had argued in *Federalist* 11, back in 1787.

Yet a powerful faction of the old Jeffersonians remained intractably opposed, and they eventually found themselves a champion in the person of Gen. Andrew Jackson. As president, Jackson vetoed a bill to recharter the Second Bank of the United States, drawing on many of the old Jeffersonian themes:

> It is to be regretted that the rich and powerful too often bend the acts of government to their selfish purposes. Distinctions in society will always exist under every just government. Equality of talents, of education, or of wealth can not be produced by human institutions. In the full enjoyment of the gifts of Heaven and the fruits of superior industry, economy, and virtue, every man is equally entitled to protection by law; but when the laws undertake to add to these natural and just advantages artificial distinctions, to grant titles, gratuities, and exclusive privileges, to make the rich richer and the potent more powerful, the humble members of society—the farmers, mechanics, and laborers—who have neither the time nor the means of securing like favors to themselves, have a right to complain of the injustice of their Government. There are no necessary evils in government. Its evils exist only in its abuses. If it would confine itself to equal protection, and, as Heaven does its rains, shower its favors alike on the high and the low, the rich and the poor, it would be an unqualified blessing. In the act before

me there seems to be a wide and unnecessary departure from these just principles.[26]

This criticism of capitalism has remained remarkably salient through American history. Sen. Ted Kennedy (D-MA) quoted from Jackson's veto message in his 1980 address to the Democratic National Convention—some 147 years after it was first delivered.

Indeed, even as we rightly dismiss the Marxist notion that capitalism impoverishes the masses for the benefit of the few—an idea that history has decisively disproved—we can and should acknowledge the challenges economic inequality poses to the republican character of our society. Wealth can and does grow, which means one person's increase does not necessitate another's decrease. But political power—the authority to guide, direct, and rule—is by its nature finite. And it is unfortunately but indubitably the case today that the wealthy and well-connected have greater access to the halls of power than the average citizen, enabling them to better understand what the government is doing and make sure their views are fully considered. Likewise, the representatives of the people too often sacrifice the public interests for their own greed. How many members of Congress leave the legislature an order of magnitude wealthier than when they arrived?

This is not a coincidence. The power of the businessman and the wealth of the legislator are demonstrations of the theorem that wealth and power are fungible. This is ultimately why Aristotle argued, some 2,400 years ago, that the best-run societies are those dominated by a middle class in which wealth is fairly equally shared. The Jeffersonian Republicans may not have understood Hamilton's economic genius, but they did understand how and why a commercialized and industrialized economy can challenge traditional notions of civic equality. These are lessons we should take to heart today, even if the Jeffersonians' anxieties about banking and debt seem backward in historical retrospect. They might not have understood how money works, but they understood how power works.

None of this means we should reject capitalism. Indeed, Friedman was fundamentally correct when he argued that economic liberty is the backbone of political liberty. The revolutionary generation, including the Jeffersonians, acceded heartily to this notion, hence their unequivocal support for private property. Yet even as the United States has built out what Hamilton had called "one great American system" of wealth, prosperity, and capitalism,[27] we too often have allowed our republican character to be corrupted. There have been and continue to be "pretorian band[s] of the Government—at once its tool & its tyrant," as Madison put it—those whose wealth purchases them power allied with those who wish to sell their power for wealth, at the expense of the public interest.[28]

A nuanced and thoughtful approach to public policy would be one in which we try to balance the protection of private property and the promotion of economic dynamism with true civic equality—and in which the government is equally disposed to consider the petitions of all citizens, regardless of how much wealth they may possess. Republicanism is still the answer.

Notes

1. Milton Friedman, *Capitalism and Freedom* (Chicago: University of Chicago Press, 2002), 59–60.

2. Virginia Declaration of Rights, § 1. This language is, of course, also rooted in John Locke's *Second Treatise of Government*.

3. Alexander Hamilton, "James Madison's Version, [18 June 1787]," Founders Online, https://founders.archives.gov/documents/Hamilton/01-04-02-0098-0003.

4. James Madison, "From James Madison to Caleb Wallace, 23 August 1785," Founders Online, https://founders.archives.gov/documents/Madison/01-08-02-0184.

5. U.S. Const. pmbl.

6. U.S. Const. art. 1, § 10, cl. 1.

7. *Federalist*, no. 10 (James Madison), https://founders.archives.gov/documents/Madison/01-10-02-0178.

8. Alexander Hamilton, "Alexander Hamilton's Final Version of the Report on the Subject of Manufactures, [5 December 1791]," Founders Online, https://founders.archives.gov/documents/Hamilton/01-10-02-0001-0007.

9. Aristotle, "Politics," in *The Complete Works of Aristotle*, ed. Jonathan Barnes (Princeton, NJ: Princeton University Press, 1984), 2:2057.

10. David Hume, "Of the Independency of Parliament," in *Political Essays*, ed. Knud Haakonssen (Cambridge, UK: Cambridge University Press, 1994), 26.

11. Cato, "General Corruption, How Ominous to the Publick, and How Discouraging to Every Virtuous Man. With Its Fatal Progress Whenever Encouraged.," in *Cato's Letters*, ed. Ronald Hamowy (Indianapolis, IN: Liberty Fund, 1995), 1:197.

12. Cato, "The Fatal Effects of the South-Sea Scheme, and the Necessity of Punishing the Directors.," in Hamowy, *Cato's Letters*, 1:43.

13. Thomas More, *Utopia*, ed. Paul Turner (New York: Penguin Books, 2003), 45.

14. Thomas Jefferson, "Thomas Jefferson's Explanations of the Three Volumes Bound in Marbled Paper (the So-Called 'Anas'), 4 February 1818," Founders Online, https://founders.archives.gov/documents/Jefferson/03-12-02-0343-0002.

15. *Federalist*, no. 11 (Alexander Hamilton), https://founders.archives.gov/documents/Hamilton/01-04-02-0163.

16. *Federalist*, no. 12 (Alexander Hamilton), https://founders.archives.gov/documents/Hamilton/01-04-02-0165.

17. Alexander Hamilton, "Report Relative to a Provision for the Support of Public Credit, [9 January 1790]," Founders Online, https://founders.archives.gov/documents/Hamilton/01-06-02-0076-0002-0001.

18. Alexander Hamilton, "Final Version of the Second Report on the Further Provision Necessary for Establishing Public Credit (Report on a National Bank), 13 December 1790," Founders Online, https://founders.archives.gov/documents/Hamilton/01-07-02-0229-0003.

19. James Madison, letter to Thomas Jefferson, July 10, 1791, Founders Online, https://founders.archives.gov/documents/Madison/01-14-02-0034.

20. James Madison, letter to Thomas Jefferson, August 8, 1791, Founders Online, https://founders.archives.gov/documents/Madison/01-14-02-0062.

21. Thomas Jefferson, letter to John Taylor, May 28, 1816, Founders Online, https://founders.archives.gov/documents/Jefferson/03-10-02-0053.

22. James Madison, "The Bank Bill, [8 February] 1791," Founders Online, https://founders.archives.gov/documents/Madison/01-13-02-0284.

23. James Madison, "For the *National Gazette*, 20 March 1792," Founders Online, https://founders.archives.gov/documents/Madison/01-14-02-0231.

24. Madison, "For the *National Gazette*, 20 March 1792."

25. James Madison, "For the *National Gazette*, 22 September 1792," Founders Online, https://founders.archives.gov/documents/Madison/01-14-02-0334.

26. Andrew Jackson, "Bank Veto Message (1832)," National Constitution Center, https://constitutioncenter.org/the-constitution/historic-document-library/detail/andrew-jackson-bank-veto-message-1832.

27. *Federalist*, no. 11 (Hamilton).

28. Madison, letter to Jefferson.

2

The American Revolution and the Pursuit of Economic Equality

CLEMENT FATOVIC

We have grown so accustomed to the phrase "American Revolution" that it is difficult to imagine an alternative label for the events that ultimately resulted in the permanent separation of 13 American colonies from Great Britain. Participants and observers had used the terms "conflict," "struggle," "resistance," "crisis," "war," and even "rebellion" to frame these events, but they were slow to adopt the term "revolution." The opposing sides had been engaged in actual combat for several years before Americans and their allies consistently began to describe what was happening as revolution.[1] Therefore, it is important to consider what Americans at the time meant—or aspired to—in calling their undertaking a revolution.

As assiduous students of political history, Americans in that period would have understood that revolutions are radical affairs.[2] The transformation of the political order from colonial dependence on an imperial monarchy an ocean away to a self-governing country resting at least nominally on the people's sovereignty was certainly a radical change. But if a change in their relationship to Great Britain was all Americans had in mind, the word "independence" would have sufficed. In adopting the word "revolution," they signaled that they were also participating in a radical transformation of the social and economic order. In other words, the American Revolution was both a political and a social revolution.

The social revolution was not a sudden development but rather, like the political events that ultimately culminated in a declaration of independence, the result of a protracted process decades in the making. Americans at the time generally understood that the political and social dimensions of the American Revolution both revolved around the idea of equality. Taking up Thomas Paine's challenge in *Common Sense* to "begin the world over again,"[3] Americans did not just seek to make themselves independent—they also set out to remake their societies.

My central claim in this chapter is that the American Revolution developed, accelerated, and expanded trends toward greater equality that had been underway for decades and inaugurated new ones that would unfold over the coming centuries, if only fitfully and still incompletely. Despite significant variations in economic and social structures among the British colonies—from the Eastern Seaboard to islands in the Caribbean and the mid-Atlantic—social relations between women and men, blacks and whites, servile and free, poor and rich, and (at least in New England) lay and clergy at the start of the century were organized hierarchically, and deeply rooted norms and habits of deference shaped relations between political leaders and their constituents.[4] Occasional and highly localized bursts of dissent did little to alter relations of subordination in vertically structured societies where the few often felt entitled to rule by virtue of their status.[5]

Even if colonists had moved away from the belief of early 17th-century Massachusetts Gov. John Winthrop that some were born "high and eminent in power and dignity, others mean and in subjection,"[6] Americans through the first half of the 18th century still generally believed that each individual belonged to an assigned place in society. By all indications, everyone seemed content to be the subject of a king even several years into the conflict with Britain. But by the time Americans settled on the label "American Revolution," they had not only renounced domination by elites in Great Britain but also begun to question the legitimacy of domination by elites at home.

The Market Revolution and Opportunities for Participation

The half century preceding independence was a period of profound social, economic, and cultural changes that altered the behaviors, relationships, attitudes, and values of individuals throughout the colonies. During this time, the colonies experienced significant upheavals that chipped away at established notions of rank and status. These changes began with the burst of religious revivalism that began in the 1730s during the Great Awakening[7] and the explosive population growth that saw the number of inhabitants increase eightfold between the start of the century and the first stirrings of colonial unrest.[8] Then an expanding capitalist economy created new opportunities for the accumulation of wealth, and consumer tastes and norms transformed, ushered in by the market revolution.[9] As reflected in bestselling literature, family portraits, and popular educational works, even relations between parents and their children were affected by these currents, as rigid notions of patriarchal authority gave way to new ideals that stressed more affectionate and egalitarian attitudes toward child-rearing.[10]

These and related developments unsettled traditional norms and roles, even if they did not necessarily undermine acceptance of hierarchy across the board. Inequalities between classes, sexes, and races would remain, but the political transformation Americans experienced forced them to reconsider the legitimacy of established ranks and traditional entitlements to rule. Although stark racial and sexual hierarchies would persist and even strengthen over the coming decades, the Revolution provoked discomfiting questions about the justifiability and terms of these relations that continue to reverberate. Likewise, the gap between the haves and the have-nots would expand after the Constitution's ratification, but the Revolution prompted Americans across class backgrounds to question the compatibility of economic inequality with republican ideals. Not only did Americans challenge long-standing assumptions that had connected status, wealth, and power, but they also pushed for and secured legal and political changes designed to ensure that the lower classes would enjoy opportunities in the economy and a voice in politics.

Scholars have been deeply divided on the relationship between class and the Revolution ever since Progressive Era historians highlighted self-serving role of propertied elites during the founding.[11] Although historians such as J. Franklin Jameson and Merrill Jensen viewed the American Revolution in more radical terms, arguing that the struggle for independence was also a "social movement" and a "war against the colonial aristocracy,"[12] political theorist Hannah Arendt praised the American Patriots for largely avoiding the "social question" that would cause other revolutions to pursue economic equality at the expense of political freedom.[13] Surveying decades of postwar scholarship on the socioeconomic context of the Revolution, Jack P. Greene found a consensus that

> far from being similar to the French Revolution, the American Revolution was a peculiarly American event in which there had been remarkably little social discontent expressed, no real social upheaval, and relatively few changes in the existing American social structure.[14]

In the past few decades, there has been an explosion of scholarship demonstrating that life on the eve of independence had been significantly transformed as a result of social and economic developments, though historians disagree on whether and how these changes might have affected attitudes toward economic equality.[15] Since the 1960s, republican revisionists, who have traced the founding's intellectual origins back to a tradition that extends from ancient Rome through the Renaissance up to the 17th- and 18th-century English commonwealth's-men, have identified egalitarian ideals animating the Revolution. For instance, Gordon S. Wood stated that "equality was in fact the most radical and most powerful ideological force let loose in the Revolution."[16]

Following the work of scholars who have examined the transformations in material culture that preceded independence, particularly the role of the so-called market revolution that modified colonists' relationships and attitudes toward commodities and each other, I argue that changes in the way colonists participated in the evolving 18th-century capitalist economy contributed to the diffusion of more egalitarian political ideals throughout the Revolution. Political events touched off by the passage of the Stamp Act in 1763 interacted with ongoing economic changes that had been underway for decades to incite a reexamination of conventional ideas and attitudes toward established forms of hierarchy. Changes in everyday economic life for ordinary colonists, from how they worked to how they consumed, had already demonstrated that social structures were fluid and adaptable. Additionally, the conscription of women, laborers, and others who had formerly been excluded from formal politics into the various boycotts stemming from nonimportation and nonconsumption movements revealed that their participation mattered.

To suggest that capitalism could contribute to egalitarian politics, even indirectly, flies in the face of both scholarly and conventional thinking. After all, the overwhelming weight of empirical evidence suggests that the long-term trend in capitalist societies is toward greater and more entrenched forms of economic inequality.[17]

However, as even its fiercest critics have pointed out, capitalism has always been a dynamic economic system capable of producing uneven and surprising effects. What Karl Marx and Friedrich Engels described as its impulse to revolutionize production and, thereby, disturb "all social conditions" is precisely what "distinguish[es] the bourgeois epoch from all earlier ones."[18] For instance, the integration of free individuals into an ever-expanding and increasingly complex international capitalist economy that created new opportunities for employment and introduced new and exciting consumer goods reshaped social relationships, engendered new cultural habits, incited fresh material desires, and lifted economic expectations.

This is by no means to suggest that individuals did not experience frustrations and disappointments or that the dynamics at work did not also pull in opposing directions. Much like industrialized forms of capitalism in the 19th century and the neoliberal variants that emerged in the closing decades of the 20th, the capitalism of the 18th-century British imperial world made it possible for a few to amass enormous fortunes off the backs of exploited laborers, whether free, indentured, or slave. Even an enthusiast for entrepreneurial pursuits such as Benjamin Franklin lamented that one of the by-products of this economic system was that "the chief Exports of Ireland seem to be pinch'd off the Backs and out of the Bellies of the miserable Inhabitants."[19] And despite the market's promise of freedom, the proliferation of what Jean-Jacques Rousseau would call "artificial needs" instigated new forms of dependence, including rising consumer debt.

However, as T. H. Breen demonstrates in his magisterial study of the market revolution, the range of increasingly affordable consumer goods, which used to be available to only those in the upper class but were now being advertised and sold to individuals of all classes, instilled a sense of "consumer choice" that made it possible for growing numbers of colonists to imagine the possibility of freedom and equality.[20]

The sense of empowerment that emerged out of this experience of a new, if narrow, form of equality in the mid-century market economy stands in stark contrast to the political powerlessness that most colonists experienced before the protests against Parliament's policies. Colonial assemblies were little more than consultative bodies tolerated by the Crown to facilitate the interests of the aristocratic elite that governed the empire as a whole.

Nevertheless, the men who served in these assemblies saw themselves perched atop a political hierarchy sanctioned by every existing source of moral authority. Scripture, tradition, and law, both natural and man-made, taught the lower orders that politics was the business of their betters. The hierarchical structure of colonial life was manifested and reinforced in virtually all social settings, from religious meetings where families were seated according to social rank to recreational pursuits that were restricted to the upper ranks.[21] Styles of dress, modes of transportation, and choices of food and drink also differed in ways that reinforced distinctions between classes. Up through the first few decades of the century at least, the sartorial choices of colonial elites set them apart in highly visible ways from their social inferiors.

But as the conflict with Great Britain unfolded, new political spaces began to open. Men in the so-called middling classes were formally permitted to participate in local elections in many colonies, but actual rates of political participation were quite low before the Stamp Act crisis. Even though it was the most prominent men in local communities who led the way in mounting the resistance to intolerable British policies, they helped mobilize and activate the participation of those who had never before gotten involved in politics or did so in only limited ways. The wealthy merchants, landowners, and professionals who represented their communities realized that boycotts organized around nonimportation and nonconsumption would not succeed without the support and participation of every consumer—including women and poorer men.

By urging ordinary men and women to give up tea, substitute homespun clothing for imported fabrics, and sacrifice other goods they had come to view as virtual necessities during the first half of the 18th century, leading Patriots initiated what Linda Kerber describes as the "politicization of the household economy."[22] Christopher Gadsden, a leading South Carolina politician and successful businessman, represented the thinking of many in urging fellow Patriots to "persuade our wives to give us their assistance, without which 'tis impossible to succeed."[23] As a result, the domestic economy became an arena for political activity, inviting the participation of those who had been largely excluded from political life.

In calling on fellow inhabitants to make resistance effective, Patriots contributed to the transformation of subjects into citizens. The new associations and assemblies that sprang up throughout the colonies, most notably the Sons of Liberty, created new political spaces for individuals who been left out of the formal channels of politics in the empire. In addition, the forms of politics that emerged made it possible for farmers, artisans, mechanics, and other laborers—including women—to participate in ways that leading political figures could not necessarily control or direct.

Despite occasional grousing by established elites, men and women, rich and poor, and professionals and laborers alike found opportunities to engage in politics by signing petitions, affixing their names to resolutions, subscribing to covenants, publishing pamphlets, raising funds and supplies for the military, and establishing organizations. And, as Breen notes, when the First Continental Congress called for the creation of the Continental Association allowing the formation of local committees to enforce nonimportation, "it has been estimated that local elections for the committees brought seven thousand men into the political process who had never before served in public office."[24] Even though women were not elected to leadership positions in the committees of safety that developed in local communities, they were called to oversee compliance with nonimportation agreements and testify against Loyalists.[25] Once these groups got involved in these ways, they would seek additional forms of participation and pressure their representatives to pursue their interests.

Certain features of the consumer economy specific to the 13 colonies made these more inclusive and participatory forms of protest possible. If existing legal and institutional rules restricted politics to provincial elites, the far more fluid and rapidly changing developments of the consumer market invited participation by virtually everyone. The breadth of that economic participation in turn made broader political participation necessary if resistance were to succeed.

Purchasing power was never even close to equal, but the possibility of participating in the consumer market as long as one had currency or goods to exchange for British imports worked to unsettle norms and patterns of conduct that had buttressed a hierarchical social order. Even if consumers differed according to their levels of disposable income (or in their ability to pay in all-too-scarce specie as opposed to bartered goods), shopkeepers interested in keeping their customers happy had to treat them with a minimum of respect.

Some retailers even highlighted the market's egalitarianism to entice would-be shoppers. In an advertisement in the *South Carolina Gazette*, one jeweler promised that all prospective consumers would be "treated in the most just and upright manner, the lowest price being fixed on each article, and those that are not judges will be served equally as if they were."[26]

The absence of legal restrictions on buying finely woven clothing and accessories, elegantly crafted porcelain tea sets, and other consumer goods that only the gentry could afford at the start of the century transformed many luxury goods into must-have items sought by the lower classes. Some manufactured British goods, such as coaches, would always be out of the reach of all but the wealthiest Americans. But as the price of certain imported goods dropped—and as more consumers became willing to purchase them on credit—the threads that had traditionally connected status and class began to unravel.

Not everyone welcomed these developments. The prospect of those in the lower ranks being able to pass themselves off as members of the upper classes elicited disapproval and condemnation. For instance, an anonymous New Englander asked readers to contemplate the horrors

> if a promiscuous use of fine cloaths be countenanced, who, that is really deserving of our respect and reverence, can be distinguished from the profligate and base born miscreant, that lies in wait to deceive under the disguise of noble garb?[27]

Similar complaints would be echoed during the Revolution by conservatives resentful of the way participation in the political realm destabilized the existing social order. Gouverneur Morris grumbled,

> These sheep, simple as they are, cannot be gulled as heretofore. In short, there is no ruling them, and now, to leave the metaphor, the heads of the mobility grow dangerous to the gentry, and how to keep them down is the question.[28]

Despite the fears of censorious elites, consumer behavior could do only so much to foster a sense of equality or empower citizens politically. Even as the market revolution worked to undermine some of the traditional cultural supports for inequality, it also created the conditions for the augmentation of material inequality. After all, the rapidly expanding trade in manufactured goods was creating new forms of wealth and privilege for shopkeepers, factors, wholesalers, and others who were savvy enough to anticipate and satisfy American consumers' ever-evolving and increasingly discerning preferences.

These developments ended up making shrewd merchants in coastal cities among the wealthiest residents in their colonies. But even as some of these large merchants and smaller retailers increased their wealth, the emerging egalitarian ethos combined with a complicated mix of religious sensibilities and republican ideals to restrain conspicuous displays of their prosperity. For instance, merchants were often encouraged to dress at the same level as their neighbors to avoid exacerbating social differences.[29]

A Society of Owners?

Consumption patterns were not the only economic factors contributing to an appreciation for equality in the years preceding the Revolution. The distribution of landownership throughout the colonies going back to the 17th century established a rough form of equality that would have profound political implications.[30] The size and productivity of landed holdings varied greatly, from small plots that barely enabled owners to eke out a living to enormous estates that allowed owners to earn fortunes from the production of rice, tobacco, and other agricultural products exported to the rest of the British world. But the differences between these extremes were overshadowed by the relatively broad distribution of ownership. Even in the lower South, where economic disparities were most extreme, substantial numbers—even outright majorities—of whites owned at least some land. In the mid-Atlantic colonies, family farms of middling size dominated the landscape.

The availability of landownership at relatively affordable rates and the prospects of achieving economic independence in the mid-Atlantic and New England colonies, at least, mitigated the development of more extreme forms of inequality and contributed to upward mobility.[31] Those who did not own land felt confident they could, and most, in fact, eventually would. That, as much as anything, tended to offset any belief in the permanence of class or status.

Contemporary scholarship generally bears out the impressions of Americans, who frequently boasted that the relative equality of landholdings set the American colonies apart from—and therefore made life there better than in—the British Isles. Franklin summed up the prevailing view among Americans:

> Land being thus plenty in America, and so cheap as that a labouring Man, that understands Husbandry, can in a short Time save Money enough to purchase a Piece of new Land sufficient for a Plantation, whereon he may subsist a Family.[32]

With land so "easily and cheaply obtained," South Carolina physician and eventual historian of the American Revolution David Ramsay asked, "who would remain in Europe, a dependent on the will of an imperious landlord, when a few years['] industry can make an independent American freeholder?"[33]

Opportunity was never perfectly equal, but it was far more equal in the American colonies than in the rest of the British colonial world—or anywhere else in Europe for that matter. For starters, legal rules concerning the sale and purchase of land in the American colonies were less restrictive than they were in Europe. Not only was land more plentiful and cheaper, but colonists did not have to contend with the same feudal laws of entail and primogeniture that propped up aristocratic elites.

Thanks to such legal rules, actual rates of landownership before independence were much higher in the American colonies than they were anywhere in Europe. Rates of landownership rarely exceeded 30 percent anywhere in Europe, but roughly 50 percent of white men in America owned real estate.[34] In some places, the numbers were much higher. In eastern New Jersey, for instance, rates of landownership among white men approached 67 percent.[35]

Many commentators at the time suggested that the wide distribution of landownership contributed significantly to the relatively high standards of living Americans enjoyed.[36] Those who traveled to or had recently moved from Europe were often struck by the stark differences in housing, attire, and food between the lower classes in the Old World compared to the New. Indeed, these differences sometimes led enthusiastic Americans to suggest (hyperbolically) a near absence of class distinctions altogether.[37]

Even if the colonies were far more stratified than many acknowledged, boastful Americans were right about one thing: America was remarkably egalitarian compared with European societies at the time.[38] Honest observers admitted that there were poor individuals and families on both sides of the Atlantic, but the availability and terms of landownership made life much more comfortable and secure in the American colonies. Indeed, the widespread ownership of property contributed to labor shortages in the mid-Atlantic and New England colonies that actually created more favorable terms of employment, leading to higher median incomes than anywhere else in the British world.[39]

To be sure, there were extraordinarily wealthy individuals in the American colonies, particularly in more established cities along the coast and in and among the slave-dependent economies of the lower South. But even the opulence of the most successful merchants and planters paled in comparison with the lifestyles of the wealthiest Europeans. Franklin's impressions are, once again, typical of Americans at the time:

> Whoever has travelled thro' the various Parts of Europe, and observed how small is the Proportion of People in Affluence or easy Circumstances there, compar'd with those in Poverty and Misery; the few rich and haughty Landlords, the multitude of poor, abject and rack'd Tenants, and the half-paid and half starv'd ragged Labourers; and views here the happy Mediocrity that so generally prevails throughout these States, where

the Cultivator works for himself, and supports his Family in decent Plenty, will, methinks, see abundant Reason to bless divine Providence for the evident and great Difference in our Favour, and be convinc'd that no Nation that is known to us enjoys a greater Share of human Felicity.[40]

Whether describing their travels through England, France, Ireland, or Spain, John Adams and Thomas Jefferson issued similar reports about the extremes of opulence and destitution that America thankfully avoided.[41]

Of course, it was one thing to celebrate what Franklin characterized as the "general happy Mediocrity that prevails"[42] in America and another to conserve it. The pursuit of equality would compete with many other interests and ideals for the attention and energy of political actors concerned first and foremost with securing political independence—not to mention avoiding the hangman's noose for treason. However, as many revolutionaries came to understand, securing the freedom, popular sovereignty, and so much else they were struggling to win would depend on securing a sufficient level of economic equality.

Republicanism and the Egalitarian Ethos

Americans knew from the republican political tradition that informed so much of their thinking that economic independence is indispensable to the free exercise of political freedom. And many viewed unchecked economic disparities as a threat to political stability. As the 17th-century English political theorist James Harrington noted, "Where there is inequality of estates, there must be inequality of power, and where there is inequality of power, there can be no commonwealth."[43]

Republicans generally agreed that economic disparities affect the capacity for political independence, but they differed over appropriate responses. They responded in one of two basic ways to the dangers of excessive economic inequality. The more aristocratic tradition, which included thinkers such as the patrician Roman orator Cicero, the Florentine historian Francesco Guicciardini, and the aforementioned Harrington, generally sought to reserve political participation for men (and it was always and only men) who possess the moral virtue and economic resources to exercise political power responsibly and resist corruption. The more democratic or populist tradition, represented by the early Roman Republican Gracchi brothers, Niccolò Machiavelli, and the English Leveler John Lilburne, not only favored the political participation of ordinary "people," understood to mean the lower classes, but proactively searched for measures designed to promote their political empowerment.[44] These include policies calculated to lift the economic fortunes of those at the bottom, strengthen those in the middle, and prevent those at the top from increasing their wealth or using it against the public interest.

Even though avowed republicans such as Adams preferred the more aristocratic alternative, the popular forms of political participation they themselves had encouraged and the growing sense of political entitlement among those who had been mobilized meant it was no longer a realistic option. As the counter-democratic backlash that ultimately led to the creation of the Constitution suggests, many elites never gave up entirely on the more aristocratic vision of republicanism.[45] But enough Americans came to embrace the second, more democratic vision of republicanism that what began as a political revolution became a social revolution.

The notion that equality was not just a general (if imprecise) condition of existing society but an aspiration that should guide policymaking for the future would be voiced from pulpits, in pamphlets, in private correspondence, at meetings, and in political orations. To varying degrees, revolutionary figures such as Jefferson, Thomas Paine, New Jersey signer of the Declaration of Independence Abraham Clark, lexicographer Noah Webster, and many others would express the conviction that economic equality was indispensable to the health of a republic. Connecticut Congregational minister and historian Benjamin Trumbull cautioned, "It will be highly politic in every free state, to keep property as equally divided among the inhabitants as possible, and not to suffer a few persons to amass all the riches and wealth of a country."[46] The only way to prevent oligarchy from gaining a foothold in the new country would be to prevent extremes of economic inequality.[47]

The pursuit of egalitarian aims in the economic sphere went hand in hand with the pursuit of equality in the political sphere. Once ordinary Americans, including poor laborers and farmers, were mobilized to engage in unconventional forms of politics, it was only natural that there would be calls to enlist them in more traditional forms of political participation. What many Americans actually did with their newfound power was to seek more of it. They started demanding greater shares of power where they had begun to acquire it and pieces of it where it was still out of reach. As Colin Bonwick notes, "Elites were forced to share their power."[48] And by changing the balance of power between Patriot elites and everyone else, the Revolution made it far more difficult for economic elites to use the reins of power to protect their wealth or prevent poorer Americans from raising their economic prospects.

Thanks to a mix of pressure from those at the bottom, a newfound commitment to the consistent application of republican ideals, and reluctant concessions from conservatives hoping to avoid further social unrest, states lowered or even eliminated property qualifications for voting and holding office. Indeed, the egalitarian impulse contributed to a variety of other changes in suffrage rules that eliminated or mitigated barriers to participation. Among other things, some states eliminated religious tests for political office, extended voting rights to anyone who served in the military, permitted free blacks to vote, and, in New Jersey, allowed wealthy women to vote.

The egalitarian spirit moved Americans to reconsider the status of individuals in other areas of life, albeit in incomplete and limited ways. The embarrassment of holding blacks in bondage throughout all 13 states as whites waged war in the name of freedom led to calls for the abolition of slavery and the end of the slave trade, even if racial prejudices among the overwhelming majority of white Americans remained largely unmoved.

Military imperatives reinforced egalitarian aims too. The gentry's inability to fill the ranks of the officer corps created opportunities for members of the lower classes to serve in positions of leadership. Alexander Hamilton, along with his friend John Laurens, went further than most in suggesting that South Carolina create three or four battalions of black soldiers, which would not only address a dire personnel shortfall but also provide black soldiers the opportunity to demonstrate their equal abilities and thereby "open a door to their emancipation."[49]

Although men of all classes generally ignored the role of women in politics—when they were not mocking the idea—women such as the author Judith Sargent Murray took it upon themselves to assert their equality and demand equal treatment in education between the sexes.[50] Married women were still subject to severe legal restrictions on the use of their property long after independence was won, but the Revolution prompted "more nearly egalitarian marital relationships" that improved the conditions of wives throughout the United States.[51]

If efforts to promote racial and sexual equality seldom resulted in meaningful legal or institutional reforms, attempts to address economic equality fared much better. In fact, the economic policies revolutionaries adopted in the first few years of the war, when republican and egalitarian energies were at their strongest, reveal a willingness to intervene in the economy and regulate the market to achieve important political objectives. Despite broad support for property rights—and concerns that overly aggressive redistributive policies could backfire if they lost the war—Americans took decisive steps to promote economic equality. From restrictions on indentured servitude to the adoption of more progressive tax codes (e.g., by eliminating poll taxes, exempting paupers from paying taxes at all, and taxing land based on its assessed value rather than its acreage), from bankruptcy reforms to the establishment of land banks that increased access to credit, legislative assemblies that now included unprecedented numbers from the middle and lower classes created policies that sought to minimize or reverse tendencies toward inequality in economic life.[52]

One of the most immediate and direct consequences for economic inequality stemmed from the confiscation of Loyalist property. The policies adopted by Patriots throughout the newly independent states provide the clearest examples of a social revolution coinciding with the political revolution. That is certainly how Loyalists themselves understood things.[53] Not only did the confiscation and sale of Loyalist property provide a much-needed source of revenue for cash-strapped governments, but it reversed the trend toward increasing economic inequality that had been developing over the preceding decades.

Because the wealthiest in many communities were Loyalists, the confiscation of their property—which in some cases got underway even before states adopted new constitutions—had the effect of removing those who skewed the distribution of wealth in ways that alarmed egalitarian republicans. Many of those who supported these confiscatory policies explicitly connected these plutocratic concentrations of wealth to the political domination they were seeking to dismantle. Although many defended these measures in frankly retributive terms or explained them in terms of military necessity, some Patriots justified these measures on openly redistributive grounds.

Both the law and actual implementation varied from one state to the next. Confiscations in most states did not do much to improve conditions for those near the bottom, but they did generally reduce concentrations of wealth at the top. In New England, Thomas Ingersoll notes, a growing anti-aristocratic ethos fueled the drive to dispossess and liquidate Loyalist property. Although the rhetoric of more radical Patriots could get overheated, threatening retribution against anyone who failed to support the Revolution, lawmakers in New England ended up limiting forfeitures to only the richest Loyalists.[54]

Even though the total number of Loyalists there who lost their property—and their homes as a result of banishment—was low (likely no more than 570 in all of New England), the amount of property that was redistributed was substantial. In Connecticut, the confiscation from just three Loyalists netted 116,000 acres.[55] Based on claims for compensation made after the Revolution, Loyalist merchants in New York representing 0.00055 percent of the population may have accounted for as much as 0.39 percent of wealth in 1774.[56] Despite its small size—and the fact that it got a late start to confiscation—Maryland eventually seized and put up for auction over 200,000 acres of land.[57] Farther south, in North Carolina, where tensions between supporters and opponents of independence were exceptionally bitter, Loyalists were subject to particularly punitive confiscations that forced many of them to leave the state for good.[58] In Georgia, just eight sales from confiscated Loyalist property captured £344,980 in the year the law went into effect.[59]

Whatever the motivations behind these policies, the results were mixed. Large holdings were divided, creating opportunities for upwardly mobile Americans to purchase land and achieve a greater measure of economic independence, but, as some had feared, the well-to-do often ended up augmenting their own wealth in a speculative frenzy that threatened to undo any egalitarian effects in the long run. In New York, "Commissioners of Sequestration" used the proceeds from seized property to assist those experiencing the privations brought on by war, such as those displaced by the British occupation of New York City.[60] In Georgia, by contrast, a legislative investigation conducted after the war found that "some Loyalist estates had been withheld from auction by the commissioners [responsible for administering the program] because prominent Whigs had already occupied them."[61] Such instances of self-dealing by those who were already wealthy and well-connected added fuel to egalitarian fires that were starting to affect fellow Patriots.

Other policies concerning private property that were intended to alleviate economic disparities fared better. There was perhaps no better example of the aristocratic system most revolutionaries sought to destroy than the feudalistic laws of entail and primogeniture that restricted the free alienation and transfer of property. As with so much else, there were variations from one colony to another. Although the law of entail generally followed antiquated English practice throughout the American colonies,[62] primogeniture laws differed significantly from one section to another, with every New England colony but Rhode Island eliminating it before the 18th century and all Southern colonies still upholding it to some degree when the Revolution began.[63]

These inheritance laws were so fundamentally incompatible with the principles of republicanism that Jefferson moved to eliminate this hold-over from feudalism in Virginia only three months after the Declaration of Independence was signed. By the time Virginia finally enacted Jefferson's proposal into law in 1785, several other states throughout the country had already revised the law.[64] Looking back on this legislative accomplishment years later, Jefferson acknowledged the egalitarian motivations behind the abolition of these outdated practices in his home state:

> The repeal of the laws of entail would prevent the accumu-lation and perpetuation of wealth in select families. . . . The abolition of primogeniture, and equal partition of inheritances removed the feudal and unnatural distinctions which made one member of every family rich, and all the rest poor, substi-tuting equal partition, the best of all Agrarian laws.[65]

Similar rationales were cited by proponents of repealing entail and primogeniture in other states. When the North Carolina legislature moved in 1784 to eliminate entails to simplify inheritance, it explicitly linked the measure to an interest in promoting "that equality of property which is of the spirit and principle of a genuine republic."[66]

For Jefferson, it was not enough to dismantle an aristocratic system of property. He sought to establish a republicanized system based on a broad distribution of property. Concerned about the dangers of the rich preying on the poor—at least among white men—Jefferson favored poli-cies throughout his career in public service that would minimize the pos-sibility of economic, and by extension political, domination. For instance, he included a radical proposal in his draft constitution for Virginia to distribute 50 acres of unused land to every free married man who had resided in Virginia for at least one year, explaining that the purpose was "the more equal Distribution of Lands, and to encourage Marriage and population." In light of the suffrage requirements he spelled out in an earlier section of that draft, the proposal would have instantly enfranchised "all male persons of full age."[67]

Another significant economic policy with redistributive effects was the issuance of paper money, which allowed citizens to make payments in the new—and rapidly depreciating—currency. Pressure to enact paper-money legislation throughout the newly independent states came most intensely from debtors, who often lacked the hard currency required to purchase consumer goods, discharge their debts, or pay their tax bills. Not all debtors were poor, and many debtors were also creditors in the complex market economy of the late 18th century. However, merchants and bankers, especially those engaged in international commerce, were vehemently opposed to paper money. Easing the financial difficulties of those struggling to pay their debts and taxes was the top priority for proponents of paper money, but equalizing the balance of economic and political power was always an important consideration too. The same was true of disputes over bankruptcy legislation, the establishment of land banks, and price controls, all of which raised the specter of class warfare.

These and related financial matters would contribute to the conservative backlash that paved the way for the creation of the Constitution. However, even many of those who would be most closely identified with this counterrevolutionary movement and spearheaded the policies that would raise alarms about an incipient oligarchy in the new republic actually supported tax policies that would minimize economic inequality.

During the 1780s, no one better represented the dangers of a new aristocracy in the United States than the wealthy Pennsylvania merchant Robert Morris, who oversaw the young nation's struggling finances as superintendent of finance starting in 1781. His establishment of the Bank of North America, which adopted deposit and loan policies that overwhelmingly advantaged prosperous merchants at the expense of land banks that generally benefited less wealthy farmers and small shopkeepers, became a symbol of the threats to republican ideals that came from fellow Americans. However, the tax policies that Morris proposed were, he argued, designed to be progressive.

Principally designed with an eye toward generating desperately needed revenue, Morris's land tax proposal was defended in republican terms as stimulating a more equal distribution of property. Noting that the burdens of a land tax would fall hardest on owners of large estates, Morris argued that the tax would incentivize these property owners to sell uncultivated land, creating new opportunities for Americans in the lower classes to provide for themselves and produce goods for sale in the marketplace. As Morris explained,

> A Land tax . . . would have the salutary operation of an Agrarian Law, without the Iniquity [of forced redistribution]. It would relieve the Indigent, and aggrandize the State, by bringing Property into the Hands of those who would use it for the Benefit of Society.[68]

Morris even justified his proposal for a poll tax as a progressive measure because the actual amount would be easy enough for the "middling Ranks" to meet and the poor were exempted from paying it altogether.[69]

Morris's protégé Hamilton similarly took a progressive approach to taxation. Not only did he condemn regressive tax policies that burdened the "common people," but he also proposed policies that exempted the poor. In a series of essays published between 1781 and 1782 recommending reforms to the fledging government, especially the need for reliable sources of revenue, the future Treasury secretary recommended a poll tax that would avoid the regressive tendencies normally associated with it. Like Morris, Hamilton argued that "the poor, properly speaking, are not comprehended" under his plan. But he went even further in promoting a luxury tax that would render the overall plan more progressive, arguing, "The rich must be made to pay for their luxuries, which is the only proper way of taxing their superior wealth."[70]

Even though there is little evidence that either Hamilton or Morris was motivated by the same republican considerations that informed the views of their more egalitarian contemporaries, their insistence that the tax policies they promoted had progressive tendencies provides additional evidence of the extent to which egalitarian ideals shaped the political culture of the Revolution.

A Durable Social Revolution

Within a few years, many political elites, alarmed by the supposed "excesses of democracy" exemplified by the egalitarian economic policies discussed above, would rally behind plans for a new constitutional system that would shift the balance of power away from states they viewed as too responsive to the demands of the lower orders toward a more powerful and centralized national government far more likely to cater to their own interests. But the constitutional counterrevolution went only so far, making important concessions to a laboring class that had grown accustomed to exercising real political power. Even though the Constitution guaranteed contracts, prohibited states from printing paper money, and implicitly codified enslaved blacks as property, it erected no property qualifications for voting or holding office, prohibited religious tests for office, allowed for the establishment of a "progressive revenue base," and included other features that upheld the Revolution's ideals of equality.[71]

Crucial to the pursuit of equality, of course, was the growing sense of being entitled to it. The notion that one deserves to be treated as an equal, under the law and in one's social relations, was a necessary precondition for the actual pursuit or achievement of equality. The demand for equality, which was first expressed politically in the cry "no taxation without representation" as a demand for equal political treatment between subjects in the American colonies and subjects in the British Isles, was made possible in part by the feeling that Americans were, in fact, in some measure, equal.

This sentiment reflected material conditions in the American colonies that differed markedly from those in Europe. The relatively broad distribution and affordability of land that went back to conditions set in the 17th century coincided with developments in the consumer marketplace of the mid-18th century to convey a sense of possibility that worked to erode some of the cultural and economic distinctions traditionally used to maintain relations of hierarchy. Though other distinctions—especially those based on artificial differences in race—would remain and harden over time, the ones that had traditionally been cited to justify class domination would be forcefully challenged once the battle for independence began. In that sense, the American Revolution was not just a repudiation of rule by hereditary elites an ocean away but also a refusal to allow aristocracy to take hold at home.

Notes

1. The word "revolution" was seldom used, except in passing, by Americans before the publication of Gouverneur Morris, *Observations on the American Revolution* (Philadelphia, PA: Styner and Cist, 1779). The term came into widespread use after a pamphlet debate between Abbé Raynal and Thomas Paine. Although Raynal used the title *The Revolution of America* for his work denouncing the "upheavals" taking place as unjustified by any injustice Americans experienced, Paine happily adopted the term in his *Letter Addressed to the Abbé Raynal on the Affairs of North-America*, rebutting the French writer's misguided and misinformed account of the struggle for independence. See Ilan Rachum, "From 'American Independence' to 'American Revolution,'" *Journal of American Studies* 27, no. 1 (April 1993): 73–81, https://www.jstor.org/stable/40464078.

2. As the etymology of the word "radical" suggests, revolutions are extreme or thoroughgoing events that go to the very roots.

3. Thomas Paine, "Common Sense," in *The Complete Writings of Thomas Paine*, ed. Philip S. Foner (New York: Citadel Press, 1945), 1:45.

4. On the varieties of stratification structuring British colonies in the 18th century, see Jack P. Greene, *Pursuits of Happiness: The Social Development of Early Modern British Colonies and the Formation of American Culture* (Chapel Hill, NC: University of North Carolina Press, 1988). On the "politics of deference" before independence, see J. G. A. Pocock, "The Classical Theory of Deference," *American Historical Review* 81, no. 3 (June 1976): 516–23, https://academic.oup.com/ahr/article-abstract/81/3/70853; and J. R. Pole, *Political Representation in England and the Origins of the American Republic*

(Berkeley, CA: University of California Press, 1966). For an overview and critique of the historiography on deference, see Richard R. Beeman, "The Varieties of Deference in Eighteenth-Century America," *Early American Studies* 3, no. 2 (Fall 2005): 311–40, https://www.jstor.org/stable/23546525.

5. On incidents of urban protest against political elites before the Revolution, see Gary B. Nash, *The Urban Crucible: Social Change, Political Consciousness, and the Origins of the American Revolution* (Cambridge, MA: Harvard University Press, 1979), 47–48, 132–33. For an example of rural protest against economic and political elites before the Revolution, see Marjoleine Kars, *Breaking Loose Together: The Regulator Rebellion in Pre-Revolutionary North Carolina* (Chapel Hill, NC: University of North Carolina Press, 2002).

6. John Winthrop, "A Model of Christian Charity," in *The Puritans in America: A Narrative Anthology*, ed. Alan Heimert and Andrew Delbanco (Cambridge, MA: Harvard University Press, 1985), 82.

7. Thomas S. Kidd, *The Great Awakening: The Roots of Evangelical Christianity in Colonial America* (New Haven, CT: Yale University Press, 2009).

8. The conditions contributing to this rapid increase in population were explored in Benjamin Franklin, "Observations Concerning the Increase of Mankind, Peopling of Countries, etc.," in *Benjamin Franklin: Writings*, ed. J. A. Leo Lemay (New York: Library of America, 1987), 367–74.

9. The market revolution continued to evolve after independence was won and was both an effect of and contributor to the political upheaval it helped shape. See John Lauritz Larson, *The Market Revolution in America: Liberty, Ambition, and the Eclipse of the Common Good* (Cambridge, UK: Cambridge University Press, 2010).

10. See Jay Fliegelman, *Prodigals and Pilgrims: The American Revolution Against Patriarchal Authority, 1750–1800* (Cambridge, UK: Cambridge University Press, 1982).

11. See, for example, Charles A. Beard, *An Economic Interpretation of the Constitution of the United States* (New York: Free Press, 1986); and Carl Becker, *The History of Political Parties in the Province of New York, 1760–1775* (Madison, WI: University of Wisconsin Press, 1909). For critiques, see Forrest McDonald, *We the People: The Economic Interpretation of the Constitution* (New Brunswick, NJ: Transaction, 1991); and Robert E. Brown, *Charles Beard and the Constitution: A Critical Analysis of "An Economic Interpretation of the Constitution,"* rev. ed. (Westport, CT: Praeger, 1979).

12. J. Franklin Jameson, *The American Revolution Considered as a Social Movement* (Princeton, NJ: Princeton University Press, 1926); and Merrill Jensen, *The Articles of Confederation: An Interpretation of the Social-Constitutional History of the American Revolution, 1774–1781* (Madison, WI: University of Wisconsin Press, 1940), 11.

13. Hannah Arendt, *On Revolution* (New York: Penguin, 1965). One of the first works to deny that the American Revolution engaged in the social "experimentation" that led to the violent "excesses" of the French Revolution was Friedrich von Gentz, *The Origins and Principles of the American Revolution Compared with the Origins and Principles of the French Revolution*, trans. John Quincy Adams (Indianapolis, IN: Liberty Fund, 2010).

14. Jack P. Greene, "The Social Origins of the American Revolution: An Evaluation and an Interpretation," *Political Science Quarterly* 88, no. 1 (March 1973): 4, https://www.jstor.org/stable/2148646.

15. See, for example, Jackson Turner Main, *The Social Structure of Revolutionary America* (Princeton, NJ: Princeton University Press, 1965); Greene, *Pursuits of Happiness*; and T. H. Breen, *The Marketplace of Revolution: How Consumer Politics Shaped American Independence* (Oxford, UK: Oxford University Press, 2004).

16. Gordon S. Wood, *The Radicalism of the American Revolution* (New York: Vintage, 1993). See also James L. Huston, *Securing the Fruits of Labor: The American Concept of Wealth Distribution, 1765–1900* (Baton Rouge, LA: Louisiana State University Press, 1998); and J. R. Pole, *The Pursuit of Equality in American History* (Berkeley, CA: University of California Press, 1978), 28, 35–36.

17. See, for example, Thomas Piketty, *Capital in the Twenty-First Century*, trans. Arthur Goldhammer (Cambridge, MA: Belknap Press, 2017).

18. Karl Marx and Friedrich Engels, *Manifesto of the Communist Party*, in *The Marx-Engels Reader*, 2nd ed., ed. Robert C. Tucker (New York: W. W. Norton & Company, 1978), 476.

19. Benjamin Franklin, letter to Thomas Cushing, January 13, 1772, Founders Online, https://founders.archives.gov/documents/Franklin/01-19-02-0007.

20. Breen, *The Marketplace of Revolution*.

21. See, for example, T. H. Breen, "Horses and Gentlemen: The Cultural Significance of Gambling Among the Gentry of Virginia," *William and Mary Quarterly* 34, no. 2 (April 1977): 239–57, https://blogs.dickinson.edu/hist-117pinsker/files/2011/01/Breen-article.pdf; and Linda L. Sturtz, "The Ladies and the Lottery: Elite Women's Gambling in Eighteenth-Century Virginia," *Virginia Magazine of History and Biography* 104, no. 2 (Spring 1996): 165–84, https://www.proquest.com/docview/195917692.

22. Linda K. Kerber, *Women of the Republic: Intellect and Ideology in Revolutionary America* (New York: W. W. Norton & Co., 1980), 41. See also Breen, *The Marketplace of Revolution*; and Mary Beth Norton, *Liberty's Daughters: The Revolutionary Experience of American Women, 1750–1800* (Ithaca, NY: Cornell University Press, 1996), 155–63.

23. Christopher Gadsden, "To the Planters, Mechanics, and Freeholders of the Province of South Carolina, No Ways Concerned in the Importation of British Manufacturers," in *The Writings of Christopher Gadsden*, ed. Richard Walsh (Columbia, SC: University of South Carolina Press, 1966), 83.

24. Breen, *The Marketplace of Revolution*, 327.

25. Kerber, *Women of the Republic*, 53–54.

26. Quoted in Breen, *The Marketplace of Revolution*, 135.

27. Quoted in Breen, *The Marketplace of Revolution*, 159.

28. Gouverneur Morris to John Penn, May 20, 1774, in Jared Sparks, *The Life of Gouverneur Morris, with Selections from Correspondence and Miscellaneous Papers* (Boston, MA: Gray and Bowen, 1832), 1:24.

29. Breen, *The Marketplace of Revolution*, 137–39.

30. On the democratic effects of broad landownership in the American colonies, see the famous account in Alexis de Tocqueville, *Democracy in America*, ed. and trans. Harvey C. Mansfield and Delba Winthrop (Chicago: University of Chicago Press, 2000), 27–55.

31. On general differences among the different sections of the North American colonies, see Greene, *Pursuits of Happiness.*

32. Franklin, "Observations Concerning the Increase of Mankind, Peopling of Countries, etc.," 368.

33. David Ramsay, "Oration on the Advantages of American Independence" (speech, Charleston, SC, July 4, 1778), https://quod.lib.umich.edu/e/evans/N28767.0001.001.

34. These figures are based on assessments later in the century, when economic inequality in the United States had started to creep back up. See Lee Soltow, *Distribution of Wealth and Income in the United States in 1798* (Pittsburgh, PA: University of Pittsburgh Press, 1989), 126.

35. Dennis P. Ryan, "Landholding, Opportunity, and Mobility in Revolutionary New Jersey," *William and Mary Quarterly* 36, no. 4 (October 1979): 571–92, https://www.jstor.org/stable/1925184.

36. Contemporary scholarship confirms this impression. See, for example, Alice Hanson Jones, *Wealth of a Nation to Be: The American Colonies on the Eve of the Revolution* (New York: Columbia University Press, 1980), 298, 340–41; and Greene, *Pursuits of Happiness*, 72–73, 91–92, 137.

37. The French American author and farmer Michel Guillaume Jean de Crèvecœur pointed to the legal rules around property to explain why "the rich and poor are not so far removed from each other as they are in Europe." Michel Guillaume Jean de Crèvecœur, *Letters from an American Farmer*, ed. Albert Stone (New York: Penguin, 1981), 67.

38. Peter H. Lindert and Jeffrey G. Williamson, *Unequal Gains: American Growth and Inequality Since 1700* (Princeton, NJ: Princeton University Press, 2016); and Peter H. Lindert and Jeffrey G. Williamson, "American Incomes Before and After the Revolution," *Journal of Economic History* 73, no. 3 (September 2013): 725–65, https://www.cambridge.org/core/journals/journal-of-economic-history/article/abs/american-incomes-before-and-after-the-revolution/F945C1180EE9D07910EEC886327CF471.

39. Greene, *Pursuits of Happiness*; and Hanson Jones, *Wealth of a Nation to Be.*

40. Benjamin Franklin, "On the Internal State of America," Franklin Papers, https://franklinpapers.org/framedVolumes.jsp?vol=43&page=781.

41. John Adams, letter to Abigail Adams, April 12, 1778, *The Adams Family Correspondence*, ed. L. H. Butterfield (Cambridge, MA: Belknap Press, 1973), 3:10; John Adams, April 6, 1778, diary entry, in *The Works of John Adams, Second President of the United States*, ed. Charles Francis Adams (Boston, MA: Little, Brown and Co., 1856), 3:121; John Adams, December 30, 1779, diary entry, in Adams, *The Works of John Adams, Second President of the United States*, 3:244; and Benjamin Franklin to Joshua Babcock, January 13, 1772, in Lemay, *Benjamin Franklin: Writings*, 873–74.

42. Franklin, "Information to Those Who Would Remove to America," in Lemay, *Benjamin Franklin: Writings*, 975.

43. James Harrington, *The Commonwealth of Oceania*, ed. J. G. A. Pocock (Cambridge, UK: Cambridge University Press, 1992), 57.

44. On the populist strain of republicanism, especially as articulated by Niccolò Machiavelli, see John P. McCormick, *Machiavellian Democracy* (Cambridge, UK: Cambridge University Press, 2011); and John P. McCormick, *Reading Machiavelli: Scandalous Books, Suspect Engagements, and the Virtue of Populist Politics* (Princeton, NJ: Princeton University Press, 2018).

45. See, for example, Clement Fatovic, *America's Founding and the Struggle over Economic Inequality* (Lawrence, KS: University Press of Kansas, 2015), 57–84. For a perspective that sees the Constitution in more egalitarian terms, see Ganesh Sitaraman, *The Crisis of the Middle-Class Constitution: Why Economic Inequality Threatens Our Republic* (New York: Vintage Books, 2017), 59–104.

46. Benjamin Trumbull, *A Discourse, Delivered at the Anniversary Meeting of the Freemen of the Town of New Haven, April 12, 1773* (New Haven, CT: 1773), 30.

47. On the republican "axioms" that guided revolutionaries on this score, see James L. Huston, "The American Revolutionaries, the Political Economy of Aristocracy, and the American Concept of the Distribution of Wealth, 1765–1900," *American Historical Review* 98, no. 4 (October 1993): 1079–105, https://www.jstor.org/stable/2166599.

48. Colin Bonwick, "The American Revolution as a Social Movement Revisited," *Journal of American Studies* 20, no. 3 (December 1986): 355–73, https://www.cambridge.org/core/journals/journal-of-american-studies/article/abs/american-revolution-as-a-social-movement-revisited/FBBA6FCA7E3783B947D191703487D9F8.

49. Alexander Hamilton to John Jay, March 14, 1779, in *The Papers of Alexander Hamilton*, ed. Harold C. Syrett (New York: Columbia University Press, 1961), 2:17–19.

50. Judith Sargent Murray, "On the Equality of the Sexes," *Massachusetts Magazine* 2 (March 1790): 132–35, https://digital.library.upenn.edu/women/murray/equality/equality.html. Though the essay was not published until after the Revolution, it was drafted in 1779.

51. Norton, *Liberty's Daughters*, 228–55.

52. Even conservatives such as Gouverneur Morris approved the notion that "taxes should be raised from individuals in proportion to their wealth." Morris, "An American: Letters on Public Finance for the *Pennsylvania Packet*," February 29, 1780, in *"To Secure the Blessings of Liberty": Selected Writings of Gouverneur Morris*, ed. J. Jackson Barlow (Indianapolis, IN: Liberty Fund, 2012), 122.

53. Many Loyalists explicitly equated republicanism with a demand for agrarian laws and other redistributive policies designed to empower the lower orders. For example, see selections from James Chalmers's *Plain Truth* and an untitled document by William Smith Jr. in Ruma Chopra, ed., *Choosing Sides: Loyalists in Revolutionary America* (Lanham, MD: Rowman & Littlefield, 2013), 87–89, 217–22.

54. Thomas N. Ingersoll, *The Loyalist Problem in Revolutionary New England* (Cambridge, UK: Cambridge University Press, 2016), 215–73. See also Richard D. Brown,

"The Confiscation and Disposition of Loyalists' Estates in Suffolk County, Massachusetts," *William and Mary Quarterly* 21, no. 4 (October 1964): 534–50, https://www.jstor.org/stable/1923305.

55. Ingersoll, *The Loyalist Problem in Revolutionary New England*, 263.

56. Edward Countryman, "The Uses of Capital in Revolutionary America: The Case of New York Loyalist Merchants," *William and Mary Quarterly* 49, no. 1 (January 1992): 11, https://www.jstor.org/stable/2947333.

57. Marcus Gallo, "Property Rights, Citizenship, Corruption, and Inequality: Confiscating Loyalist Estates During the American Revolution," *Pennsylvania History: A Journal of Mid-Atlantic Studies* 86, no. 4 (Autumn 2019): 474–510, https://www.jstor.org/stable/10.5325/pennhistory.86.4.0474.

58. John R. Maass, "'The Cure for All Our Political Calamities': Archibald Maclaine and the Politics of Moderation in Revolutionary North Carolina," *North Carolina Historical Review* 85, no. 3 (July 2008): 251–81, https://journals.scholarsportal.info/details/00292494/v85i0003/251_cfaopcomirnc.xml.

59. Robert G. Mitchell, "The Losses and Compensation of Georgia Loyalists," *Georgia Historical Quarterly* 68, no. 2 (Summer 1984): 233–34, https://www.jstor.org/stable/40581224.

60. For more details, see Howard Pashman, "The People's Property Law: A Step Toward Building a New Legal Order in Revolutionary New York," *Law and History Review* 31, no. 3 (August 2013): 587–626, https://www.cambridge.org/core/journals/law-and-history-review/article/abs/peoples-property-law-a-step-toward-building-a-new-legal-order-in-revolutionary-new-york/2AF0DEB3413D98C14DFF3C3BD24436ED.

61. As a result, the distribution of property ownership before and after the confiscation program remained more or less the same. Robert S. Lambert, "The Confiscation of Loyalist Property in Georgia, 1782–1786," *William and Mary Quarterly* 20, no. 1 (January 1963): 89, 94, https://www.jstor.org/stable/1921356.

62. On the complicated theory and law of inheritance in the 18th-century British world and how the revolutionary generation transformed it, see Stanley N. Katz, "Republicanism and the Law of Inheritance in the American Revolutionary Era," *Michigan Law Review* 76, no. 1 (November 1977): 1–29, https://repository.law.umich.edu/cgi/viewcontent.cgi?article=3901&context=mlr.

63. John V. Orth, "After the Revolution: 'Reform' of the Law of Inheritance," *Law and History Review* 10, no. 1 (Spring 1992): 35–36, https://www.jstor.org/stable/743813. The near absence of primogeniture laws in New England was one reason John Adams thought an oligarchy was unlikely to form in that part of the country, stating "the tendency of the laws of inheritance [in New England] is perpetually to distribute and subdivide whatever portion of land acquires any great market value." John Adams, *A Defence of the Constitutions of the United States of America*, in Adams, *The Works of John Adams*, 4:359–60.

64. Holly Brewer, "Entailing Aristocracy in Colonial Virginia: 'Ancient Feudal Restraints' and Revolutionary Reform," *William and Mary Quarterly* 54, no. 2 (April 1997): 307–46, https://www.academia.edu/40474992/Entailing_Aristocracy_in_Colonial_Virginia_Ancient_Feudal_Restraints_and_Revolutionary.

65. Thomas Jefferson, *Autobiography*, in *The Works of Thomas Jefferson*, ed. Paul Leicester Ford (New York: G. P. Putnam's Sons, 1904–05), 1:68. Jefferson's condemnation of the "unnatural" features of these laws echoed critiques in popular mid-century novels that extolled the virtues of more egalitarian family relations. See Fliegelman, *Prodigals and Pilgrims*, 51–53.

66. Orth, "After the Revolution," 41–42. Promoting equality along one dimension sometimes undermined it along another: Equalizing the inheritance rights of children came at the expense of the dower rights of widows, who lost the third share to which they had formerly been entitled. See Kerber, *Women of the Republic*, 146.

67. Thomas Jefferson, *The Papers of Thomas Jefferson*, ed. Julian Boyd (Princeton, NJ: Princeton University Press, 1950), 2:139–40.

68. Quoted in Fatovic, *America's Founding and the Struggle over Economic Inequality*, 48.

69. For more details about Morris's tax plans, see Fatovic, *America's Founding and the Struggle over Economic Inequality*, 47–49.

70. Quoted in Fatovic, *America's Founding and the Struggle over Economic Inequality*, 120. Despite his reputation as an unapologetic plutocrat, an examination of Hamilton's tax proposals at both the state and national levels reveals a consistent effort to shift tax burdens to the wealthy and relieve, if not eliminate, burdens on the poor. See Fatovic, *America's Founding and the Struggle over Economic Inequality*, 119–24.

71. For an overview of the Constitution's egalitarian dimensions, see Sitaraman, *The Crisis of the Middle-Class Constitution*.

3

Economic Causes and Consequences of the American Revolution

DEIRDRE NANSEN MCCLOSKEY

How can we weigh the costs and benefits of the American Revolution? Even if we tried to do so in material terms, we would have to begin by considering the revolt's sheer human scope. War is hell, and the American Revolution began with a society-wide war.

Historians of the events from the Boston Tea Party in 1773 through Yorktown in 1781 and the Treaty of Paris in 1783 agree the Revolution was a civil war—the first of two shooting wars determining how Americans would govern themselves. According to the conventional account of the combatants in this first civil war, in 1780 about a third of the roughly 2,100,000 free citizens of the British colonies that became the United States would have described themselves, with mixed idealism and self-interest, as Patriots.[1] Another third were loyal to the British Empire.

Threatened with being tarred and feathered, having their property seized, and worse, about 60,000 of the roughly 700,000 Loyalists had decamped to Canada or Britain by 1783.[2] The decamping is noteworthy and considerably affected Canadian history, but it was nowhere close to the entire group. The 91 percent of Loyalists who lingered into the early republic perhaps found their voice as conservative moderates restraining their fellow citizens' wilder democratic impulses. The final third of the colonists occupied the uneasy middle—what we have come to call in American politics the independents. They were not willing to pledge their lives, fortunes, and sacred honor to a bloody, collective exit from the British Empire or a fierce, and also bloody, loyalty to king and country.

Historians calculate that 25,000 to 70,000 Patriots died directly because of the war, killed by camp fever and musket fire. Some 7,000 Loyalists did too. An additional 130,000 Americans were killed by a spike in smallpox that the movement of populations during the war exacerbated.[3] The war, in other words, was seriously disruptive due to the death, injury, disease, property damage, territorial occupations, and naval blockades it caused.

In America's other civil war, from 1861 to 1865, 1.8 percent of the country's combined population—Northerners and Southerners, free and enslaved—died as soldiers, and doubtlessly, numerous civilians in the South died during the suppression of the rebellion.[4] But during the first civil war, even setting aside deaths from smallpox and taking the lower estimate of Patriot soldiers' deaths, when we combine that number with Loyalists' deaths, we find that nearly as many died relative to the population as in the second civil war: fully 1.5 percent of merely the free Americans in 1776. Compared with the guillotining of French nobles and prison deaths from maltreatment during the French Revolution's Reign of Terror, in the American Revolution, fully 11 times more soldiers died relative to the population at risk. (In France, of course, Napoleon Bonaparte later vastly extended the slaughter.)

Taking the higher 75,000 figure for Patriots' war deaths in the American Revolution would imply that such deaths alone amounted to almost 4 percent of the free population. By comparison, about one-third of 1 percent of the American population died in World War II.[5] The Revolution was assuredly a bloody business. Its human cost was very high.

But was it a profane, *mere* "business" or a holy, sacred devotion? What can we make of the material and economic arguments for the Revolution? And what can we say about its implications for the former colonies' prosperity?

An Inner Revolution

Did economic burdens cause the American Revolution? Contrary to the indignant rhetoric of the Declaration of Independence, historians have long realized that the Revolution's narrow economic causes were trivial. As the economic historian Ben Baack summarizes, until the triumphant conclusion in 1763 of the Seven Years' War against France—so costly to the Crown in Parliament, if gratifyingly successful for the British Empire—

> there was little, if any, reason to believe that one day the American colonies would undertake a revolution. . . . As a part of the [British] Empire the colonies were protected from foreign invasion [and the Native Americans allied with the French]. . . . In return, the colonists paid relatively few taxes and could engage in domestic economic activity without much interference [and had done so for a century]. . . . The colonists were only asked to adhere to . . . the Navigation Acts [which had been in place since the late 17th century and] required that all trade within the Empire be conducted on ships . . . constructed, owned, and largely manned by British citizens. Certain enumerated goods whether exported [such as tobacco] or imported [such as sugar] by the colonies had to be shipped through England, regardless of the final port of [origin or] destination.[6]

But after the Seven Years' War, an exhausted treasury drove the British to try novel policies on the American colonials, which mightily irritated the latter.

In the Proclamation of 1763 and the Quebec Act of 1774, for example, Parliament ordered the colonists not to trade with the British allies among the First Nations in the massive lands conquered from the French or to settle there. More famously, Parliament moderately taxed the colonists to pay for protection from those very Indians and European invaders from the west and to retrospectively pay the debt incurred during the French and Indian War (as the colonists called it).

Yet Baack reports that the estimate historians from the 1940s to the 1970s arrived at using various methods "suggests the per capita *tax* burden in the colonies ranged from two to four per cent of that in Britain."[7]

(Emphasis added.) The sum was paltry. For example, though the notorious Stamp Act of 1765 was lower than similar taxes in Britain and was soon abandoned, its annual revenue would have handily paid for the ongoing cost of the 10,000 troops stationed in British forts in the American West. But unreasonably, the colonists were aroused to political, though not yet military, action against even this light impost, organizing successful boycotts of British goods. Britain repealed the Stamp Act the next year.

In other words, Parliament's moderate and often short-lived taxes after 1763, though they caused political kerfuffles, had hardly enough *economic* impact to inspire *military* patriotism. The colonists, whom the British Crown had for a century left to their own devices and whose land was much more densely populated with Europeans than the French lands to the north, were determined to act as economic free riders. After 1789, indeed, the new nation would tax *itself* more steeply than any British Parliament had proposed.

"No taxation without representation" raised the political temperature during the 1760s and 1770s, but it was not in material terms a revolt-worthy burden. After all, in Britain, the poor were taxed on their beer without any representation. And before Parliament was reformed, the United Kingdom's many big cities, newly thronged, were grossly underrepresented, while old and empty towns were grossly overrepresented. Yet the British were not moved to take up arms against their sea of troubles.

The other economic irritation, the Navigation Acts from the 1660s, could have been a significant burden. But though foreign trade plays an outsized role in historical accounts because it is easy to measure, it was always a modest share of the colonial economy. The colonials got their bread, meat, houses, and childcare and most of their furniture at home—from other Americans or by their own handiwork. A regulatory distortion of tobacco and lumber exports or tea and wine imports, therefore, would not radically impoverish the colonials. The more radical impoverishment would come from the war's radical distortions.

The Navigation Acts, in any case, had been in law for a century and were by no means a novel irritation. Under the rules (if they were enforced against smugglers), Virginian exports of tobacco, for example, had to go through English ports in Bristol or London on British ships before entering the big markets of Amsterdam. The extra trip reduced the price of tobacco that colonial planters received. Following the money, the lost revenues in Virginia especially annoyed precisely those Virginians who became most active in the Revolution.[8]

The general scope of the burden is easily calculated, at any rate. One simply compares prices in Amsterdam with those in London and Virginia. As for the post-1763 taxation, historians have concluded that the burden from the Navigation Acts was at most a mere 1 percent of colonial income.[9] And colonial smuggling of the enumerated products, especially in coastal trade, made the Navigation Acts to some degree dead letters among the colonies. For instance, Virginians could get away with smuggling tobacco to Boston or Jamaica.

The counterfactual scenarios of full enforcement of the Navigation Acts versus complete exemption from the tax provide another reason to view the calculations as an upper bound on the actual economic burden. And that bound is low. It was hardly enough, in sober reality (if sober reality is what we are talking about), to make it "necessary for one people to dissolve the political bands which have connected them with another."

One might argue that, in the heated atmosphere of the late 1760s and early 1770s, the Patriots feared that Parliament's on-and-off impositions presaged, as the Declaration put it, "the establishment of an absolute tyranny over these States" as a "direct object," meaning that *future* taxes and restrictions were the worry.[10] But such a minatory argument could apply to any change of any policy anywhere and at any time, creating a rational or irrational expectation of tyrannical extensions of any act by any state. If this argument held weight, revolutions would break out everywhere weekly.

On the contrary, as even the Declaration admitted, "Prudence, indeed, will dictate, that governments, long established, should not be changed for light and transient causes." True, the Patriots said they had terrifying expectations. But their expectations were not soberly rational in view of the experience of, say, the Canadians, who did not stage a revolution.

In short, a Marxist or economistic supposition that material interests always drive history does not explain the American Revolution. In 1913, the progressive historian Charles Beard traced the 1789 Constitution to allegedly self-interested and corrupt economic origins. Most historians since then have demurred,[11] though in 2002, the economic historian Robert McGuire mounted a persuasively quantitative defense of Beard's economistic assignment of motives.[12]

However, an entire school of Marxist historians has adhered to an economistic cynicism similar to Beard's, identifying, for example, a commercial revolution during the early republic after the break with Britain. Charles Sellers's influential book *The Market Revolution: Jacksonian America, 1815–1846* characterized an allegedly novel respect for the bourgeoisie in America after the Revolution as a fresh plague that would "wrench a commodified humanity to relentless competitive effort and poison the more affective and altruistic relations of social reproduction that outweigh material accumulation for most human beings."[13]

But this implied view of prerevolutionary America, though it lives on in leftist historiography, is mistaken. The Atlantic economy was unified, as was its ideology. In 1723, the Americans were already, like their English cousins, "a polite and commercial people,"[14] as William Blackstone described the English in his *Commentaries on the Laws of England*—a book studied closely by every legally minded American.

No one can read Benjamin Franklin's account of his escape in 1723 from a traditional apprenticeship to his brother or his later economic success in Philadelphia—not to mention the facts and expressions in the colonists' wills and probate inventories revealing a commercial mentality—and suppose prerevolutionary Americans lived in closed, corporate communities without an ideological commitment to property, trade, and innovation.[15] After all, the Patriots complained precisely about British interference in a market economy, in which they implied they would happily swim if evil old George III would let them. The American economy by 1776 had been long and self-consciously capitalist (or would have been, if that scientifically inaccurate word had been coined so early). It had been so since the second generation of settlers, even in pious Plymouth, Massachusetts. Capitalism had already happened in America.

No, as historian Bernard Bailyn demonstrated in the 1960s and as prior and subsequent historians' calculations confirmed by showing the implausibility of economic burdens as an efficient cause, the Revolution's origins lay not in material burdens but in a liberal ideology long grown up in the colonies. Bailyn wrote in 1960,

> The modernization of American politics and government during and after the Revolution took the form of a sudden, radical realization of the program that had first been fully set forth by the [British] opposition intelligentsia . . . in the reign of George the First [1714–27]. . . . Americans driven by the same aspirations but living in a society in many ways modern, and now [as they conceived] released politically, could [in 1776 and in the Revolution's denouement in 1789] suddenly act. Where the English opposition had vainly agitated for partial reforms . . . American leaders [by 1789] moved swiftly and with little social disruption to implement systematically the outermost possibilities of the whole range of radically libertarian ideas.[16]

Bailyn was being precise. His "libertarian ideas" were true liberalism (and still are). To imitate at some length his admirable precision, one must say further that the Revolution's ideological cause was *not*, as is often vaguely claimed without much precise reflection, the Enlightenment.

The Enlightenment was undoubtedly a fine thing, resulting in the science and reason that we all admire and the deism and atheism that some of us do not. But like the Renaissance three centuries earlier and the Scientific Revolution two centuries earlier, the 18th-century Enlightenment was mainly the hobby of a tiny elite. The Renaissance, Scientific Revolution, and Enlightenment contrast sharply with the utterly novel egalitarianism of 18th-century liberalism.

The Enlightenment and its follow-on had little or nothing to do with consent of the governed, constitutionalism, equality of permission, and liberal democracy. After all, the leading tyrants of the time were notably enlightened. Catherine the Great was a tyrant over serfs and the noble service class, sitting in Saint Petersburg with her court full of mathematicians and musicians. And Thomas Jefferson was a tyrant over his slaves, lying in Monticello with French wine on the bedroom side of his bed and expensively imported books on the study side. Frederick the Great, who even Immanuel Kant could not claim was a liberal, was a great-ish composer of symphonies still listened to and an expert flute player.

In a letter to John Adams in March 1776, Abigail Adams asked whether the gentry of Virginia—namely, the enlightened Jefferson, James Madison, and George Washington—were lords "and the common people vassals." Of the Virginians, she was

> ready to think the passion for Liberty cannot be . . . Strong in the Breasts of those who have been accustomed to deprive their fellow Creatures of theirs. . . .
>
> [Enslavement] is not founded upon that generous and christian principle of doing to others as we would that others should do unto us.[17]

From England the year before, Samuel Johnson had pointedly asked likewise of the American traitors to the Crown, "How is it that we hear the loudest yelps for liberty among the drivers of negroes?"[18]

Liberal equality of *permission*, that is, was nothing like an entailment of the Enlightenment, as one can see in Kant's short 1784 essay "What Is Enlightenment?" Kant calls liberty of *conscience* the sole characteristic of enlightenment. Like Georg Wilhelm Friedrich Hegel and other German professors, he furthermore excuses members of the Prussian aristocracy for keeping their official positions. It is easy to imagine modern science and an alleged rule of reason implementing the most hideously illiberal tyranny. Indeed, from Plato to George Orwell, the authors of many utopias and dystopias have imagined just that, and many modern mega-states have implemented such tyrannies.

European uber-enlightened rationalists such as Auguste Comte, Karl Marx, and Jean Jacques Rousseau stood explicitly against the British and American liberalism we are construing here. What was notable about the liberal experiment after 1776, said Alexis de Tocqueville about America and John Stuart Mill about Britain, was its egalitarianism, its equality of permission. The Enlightenment featured no such egalitarianism. At length, an enlightened if illiberal German chemistry invented mustard gas and Zyklon B, and Soviet rulers, with their enlightened appreciation for classical music and the rational science of historical materialism, invented illiberal central planning enforced by gulags.

The cause of the Revolution, then, was a specifically liberal ideology, not the Enlightenment or material burdens and interests. When the idealistic and highly successful American Maj. Gen. Benedict Arnold grew disgusted in 1780 with what he considered his fellow Patriots' material self-dealing, he shifted to an equally fierce loyalty to the Crown. Idealists routinely make such leaps, in contrast with independents, who are willing to go along to get along.

We are liable after Marx and positivism to suppose, cynically and Beard-like, that all motivation is economic, a matter of getting along materially. We are all historical materialists now. But as even some Marxists and a few utilitarian economists acknowledge, economic interest is not the only human motivation, and it is commonly not dispositive. Men followed Washington for reasons other than their pocketbooks.

Humans, in other words, march also to the music of the transcendent, whether good, indifferent, or evil—God or baseball or the Thousand-Year Reich. True, the American Revolution spilled blood and spent fortunes, while the Patriots claimed economic burdens made the violence necessary. The Declaration is full of such rhetoric, calculated to appeal (one supposes) to the outer, material interests of persuadable independents.

But if the Revolution's cause was always partially outer, its greater cause and lasting effect were inner—it brought an entirely new idea of equality of permission into a world that had been, since the coming of agriculture, under an ancient and naturalized hierarchy. Jefferson the enslaver's clause about all men being created equal was by 1776 a commonplace among advanced liberal thinkers, mainly those in Britain and America and a few of those in France. In the same revolutionary year, Adam Smith (who, like Edmund Burke, was sympathetic to the colonists) wrote,

> All systems either of preference or of restraint [such as the Navigation Acts], therefore, being thus completely taken away, the obvious and simple system of natural liberty establishes itself of its own accord. Every man, as long as he does not violate the laws of justice, is left perfectly free to pursue his own interest his own way, and to bring both his industry and capital into competition with those of any other man, or order of men. The sovereign is completely discharged from . . . the duty of superintending the industry of private people, and of directing it towards the employments most suitable to the interest of the society.[19]

To be sure, the liberal idea of equality of permission had been articulated before its heyday in the 18th century, but seldom, and it had come under violent attack from ancient royalists, as it is today by modern statists. In 1381, the defrocked priest John Ball was hanged, drawn, and quartered in St. Albans, England, for asking, "When Adam delved and Eve span, / Who was then the gentleman?"[20] A century before the Patriots' victory in America, the English Leveler Richard Rumbold declared from the scaffold at his own public hanging, "I am sure there was no man born marked of God above another; for none comes into the world with a saddle on his back, neither any booted and spurred to ride him."[21]

Back in 1685, few in the crowd that gathered in Edinburgh, Scotland, for the entertainment of seeing the Leveler hanged by James II's servants would have agreed with Rumbold's liberal and anti-hierarchical declaration. A century later, a few more would agree, prominently Smith. By 1985, virtually everyone would agree, in theory if not in practice.

In short, the outer American Revolution of violence, initiated at the Battles of Lexington and Concord against the redcoats on April 19, 1775, was ideological in cause: It came from an inner revolution of a liberal equality of permission into which the varied colonies had been drifting since they were founded.

Yet one material and powerful cause that led to the liberal drift was the necessary lack of intrusive central authority from London in an age of sailing, when a message took a month to arrive from across the Atlantic and did so with high and perilous variance. It got the American colonists—at least the white men of property discussing matters in New England town meetings or Virginia's House of Burgesses—into the habit of self-rule. Contrary to myths of Roman, Chinese, or Ottoman centralization, loose governance from the metropolis was historically typical before the telegraph, steamship, airplane, and bureaucracies and secret police enforcing the will of a colonial office or politburo. The political scientist James Scott and the historian James Searing observed that before these modern devices of state capacity, every state had trouble governing people at the margins of its dominion—highlanders, colonials, and the like—so such people were relatively liberated compared to subjects in the metropolis.[22]

War and Wealth

So much for the Revolution's material and ideological causes. What of its effects?

The Revolution's economic consequences were not in the short run what the Patriots' eloquence had promised. The too-loose confederation before the new Constitution of 1789 was an economic embarrassment. The separate states erected tariffs as barriers against each other's exports and quarreled over pensions and bonded debts from the war. The confederation's one great economic accomplishment was the Northwest

Ordinance of 1787, which, along with a few earlier enactments, ended disputes among the states about western claims and laid out the procedure for settling the vast area south of Canada, east of the Mississippi, and north of the Ohio River that the British had ceded in the Treaty of Paris.

An economic crux in the 1789 Constitution that replaced the confederation's arrangement was the agreement to forbid states from erecting tariffs against each other, like those among the states of India and in Europe before the European Union, which remain in force today. Constructing thereby a great free-trade area forced Americans to compete with each other in exertion and innovation, greatly benefiting the average worker and consumer. The authority to impose an external tariff, which the Constitution granted to the federal government, immediately became the main source of federal income and a political football for protecting northern textile mills and, later, steel mills. Yet so large was the nation—doubled by the Northwest Territory, redoubled by the Louisiana Purchase, and then supplemented in 1848 by the seizure of half of Mexico—that the external tariff's economic harms remained small relative to gross domestic product.[23]

The large scale of the open market created by the Revolution and its aftermath, then, was good for business. Yet that scale would have been still larger if the Americans had stayed in the British Empire, especially when, in 1846, the UK began free trade with the world. The United States' federal system did not in the long run prevent the states from enacting the economic equivalent of state-level tariffs through state-level labor laws, occupational licensure requirements, local zoning, and the banking regulations that led to the bizarrely high number and instability of American banks. Government policy, not private monopolies or commercial greed, has always been the main obstacle to economic progress.

But in 1783, progress from the vast geographical scope for private competition and innovation lay far in the future. For Americans huddled on the East Coast tidewater, the Revolution's biggest short-run economic consequence was a shocking drop in income, as the economic historians Jeffrey Williamson and Peter Lindert show, confirming earlier work by James Shepherd and Gary Walton in 1976.[24] Keynesian fantasy sometimes sees war as a salubrious economic stimulus. War has seldom been so. It usually turns out that killing people and being killed, burning most houses, blockading every trading ship, and diverting labor and capital to toss them away in war is not a good plan for economic progress.

The Keynesian stimulus that the United States created through its war effort after 1939 as the "arsenal of democracy" and after December 7, 1941, as a combatant nation is conventionally thought to have permanently solved the Great Depression. It did so temporarily and, of course, only until 1945—after which, if the Keynesian premise were true, the Depression should have returned with a vengeance as millions of former servicemen sought civilian work and as government war spending abruptly ceased. Though many economists feared this would happen, it didn't. Innovation, not spending, enriches. And the innovations attributed to the pressure of armed struggle are usually irrelevant to the arts of peace.

In 1776, a peaceful pattern of activity, such as joining Canada in loyalty to Britain, would have stimulated innovation in something other than cannons and warships. In fact, America's Revolutionary era was sterile in terms of innovation. Cotton gins and steamboats came later. War is hell, not a path to economic heaven.

Williamson and Lindert's dismal estimates imply that America's real income per capita dropped by over a fifth between 1774 and 1800. They note that "America's urban centres were damaged by British naval attacks, by their occupation, and by the eventual departure of skilled and well-connected Loyalists." To this they add a burden from "the disruptions to overseas trade during the revolution and, after 1793, the Napoleonic Wars." A path for the new nation akin to Canada's would have kept the colonial merchants and Loyalist labor within the economic ambit of the greatest naval power facing Napoleon, instead of outside.

"The most painful of these shocks," Williamson and Lindert continue, "was the loss of well over half of all trade with England between 1771 and 1791. In addition, America lost Imperial bounties like those on the South's indigo and New England's whale oil." The Navigation Acts were by no means disadvantageous only to Americans. "Without the 1774–1790 economic disaster," the authors conclude, "America might well have recorded a modern economic growth performance even earlier, perhaps [becoming] the first on the planet to do so."[25]

The economic liberalism growing in the Anglosphere was led intellectually by Scots during the 18th century but practically by Americans during the 19th century. Americans were trivial contributors to enlightened science until about 1900. On that score, they remained not much to write home about until the intellectual migrants from *Mitteleuropa* flooded in during the era of fascism and World War II. Yet the uniquely British liberalism of America's society and economy resulted, after the quarter century of decline from the Revolution's immediate effects, in massive mechanical and biological inventions: cotton gins, steamboats, mechanical harvesters, sewing machines, gun making with interchangeable parts, and selective breeding of cotton plants that quadrupled yields.

These economic successes of what Smith called in 1776 "the obvious and simple system of natural liberty" were not, as Smith thought and many economists still believe, merely a function of better resource allocation. Yes, cutting off trade could cause per capita income to fall by one-fifth. But the Great Enrichment that began in the early 19th century in the Anglosphere and spread to much of the globe did not involve gains or losses of 20 percent from good or bad allocation; rather, it brought gains on the order of 2,500 percent from innovation.[26]

Good resources, like timber, fish, and soil, were likewise not what made America rich, as one can see in the enrichment of resource-poor places like Japan and Hong Kong and the poverty of resource-rich places like Russia and Congo. Nor, contrary to the neo-institutionalist argument that the World Bank still espouses, were American and British property or contract laws much superior to those of other places.

Good allocation of existing resources is a fine idea that gets you 10 percent, 20 percent, or even 100 percent improvement—once. Splendid. But Britain's radical innovations of steam and steel, the United States' corporate form, Germany's modern university, and, above all, the encouragement to take economic risk explain the Great Enrichment's greatness—that transformative 2,500 percent. As Tocqueville wrote in 1835,

> Looking at the turn given to the human spirit in England by political life; seeing the Englishman . . . inspired by the sense that he can do anything . . . I am in no hurry to inquire whether nature has scooped out ports for him, or given him coal or iron.[27]

Slavery is further fodder for informing counterfactual histories. If America had remained under Britain, the British Empire's abolition of slavery after 1833 through compensated emancipation might have become *une cause d'indépendance* in the minds of American slaveholders, dividing the North from Virginia and North Carolina in the manner of Upper and Lower Canada. During the decades before America's second civil war, alas, slaveholders refused similar schemes proposed by moderate abolitionists.

Yet in a Canada-type counterfactual scenario, the Southerners in the 1830s would have lacked the alliance with New England radicals that they possessed in 1776 and even 1787. They might therefore have settled for the pounds sterling of monetary compensation. Their fellow enslavers in the British Caribbean did.

Similarly, in 1861, Czar Alexander II decreed that Russian private holders of serfs must liberate them for redemption payments imposed on the freedmen. This scheme was like granting American freedmen 40 acres and a mule but burdening them with a lifetime obligation to pay for the grant. Yet that would have been better than a second civil war.

In any case, the existing international comparisons show that, contrary to the view that new historians of slavery like Sven Beckert popularized in the 1619 Project, slavery was not the source of American enrichment. If it were, then Canada—where descendants of Underground Railroad fugitives still live in Windsor, Ontario, across from Detroit, Michigan—would have lagged in economic growth during the Great Enrichment. It did not.

We cannot ignore Abraham Lincoln's noble words in his second inaugural address:

> If God wills that [the war] continue until all the wealth piled by the bondsman's two hundred and fifty years of unrequited toil shall be sunk, and until every drop of blood drawn with the lash shall be paid by another drawn with the sword, as was said three thousand years ago, so still it must be said "the judgments of the Lord are true and righteous altogether."[28]

But, like the heated rhetoric of the Declaration of Independence fourscore and nine years earlier, Lincoln's soaring poetry should not be considered a proper economic analysis, any more than the 1619 Project could be.

In the Canada-style counterfactual scenario, the historical pressure from the radical democracy that the rhetoric of Jefferson and especially Thomas Paine promised in 1776 would have been replaced by the gradual liberalization that was already creeping into British politics and was transferred to Canada in 1867—the same year many workingmen in the UK were democratically enfranchised. One could ask how much the UK's liberalization was a reaction to threatening models of popular rule in France and the United States, of course. The extraction of Mexico, Bolivia, and Brazil from Spanish and Portuguese colonial rule did not cause these countries to develop as poster children for successful liberalism.

But the United States, especially after it settled in 1865 the worst of its sins against the liberal ethos, was such a model, though with hideous exceptions down to the present. The United States—guaranteed by Lincoln's generals to be a unified polity that was democratic in principle, if not always in practice—probably put pressure on European politics by its example. Yet the French Revolution and the British Reform Acts surely continued to exert the strongest pressure in a liberal direction. After all, Alexander II liberated the serfs before Lincoln liberated the slaves, not after. The czar doubtless had European, not American, models in mind, especially the modernizing policies of successful autocrats, such as the Prussian king's emancipation of the serfs in 1807.

In 1780, a year and a half before the Battle of Yorktown settled the issue, Adams, John Hancock, and 60 others looking forward to the new nation founded, on the model of the Royal Society back in London, the American Academy of Arts and Sciences. The Latin motto on its seal is still *sub libertate florent*, "under liberty they flourish." And so under *libertas* they eventually did flourish, because after 1776, more and more people were gradually emancipated to exercise equality of permission, with its astounding material and spiritual fruit.

That was the lasting economic consequence of the American Revolution. Eventually, it yielded a society, polity, and economy of, by, and for the people. And in time, it even yielded the promise of an entire world of, by, and for the people. That was the economic and transcendent significance of the American Revolution.

Sub Libertate Florent

The American Revolution's most significant economic consequences were therefore not above all economic—and neither were they simple or straightforward.

The United States' independence advanced the democratic ideal worldwide but left the issue of slavery hanging. It advanced economic liberalism as an ideology but opened the doors of Congress to protectionism. It advanced the revolutionary ideal of "Don't tread on me" but confirmed the busybody impulse from early colonial times of attaching a scarlet letter to any social deviant. It disestablished the Anglican church in Virginia and the Congregational church in Massachusetts but witnessed Great Awakenings that inspired policy lurches impossible in Britain or Canada.

In 1819, the Swiss politician Benjamin Constant articulated a distinction between "ancient" and "modern" liberty.[29] Ancient liberty is the right to participate in a polity—to gather in Athens and debate the expedition to Syracuse or to carry a shield in the phalanx. Its form after the rise of nationalism became self-determination.

Modern liberty, by contrast, is an individual's right to be left alone by the polity. A New Englander could be proud of participating in the town meeting, as exhibited in Norman Rockwell's famous painting for the *Saturday Evening Post* illustrating the freedom of speech, the first of Franklin D. Roosevelt's "four essential human freedoms."[30] But the town meeting and Roosevelt's further promise of freedom from *want* entailed numerous gross violations of *modern* liberty. "Banned in Boston" became a watchword for even the liberty-mad New Englanders' coercion of others. Modern liberty may not have required a revolution of self-determination.

What modern liberty did require was the idea of equal liberty—not equal outcomes, as in socialist thought since 1848, or equal opportunity, as in the so-called new liberal thought of the past century and a half, but the equal *permission* that Americans since colonial times increasingly claimed as their due. A naive European newly arrived in America in the late 19th century asked a man in the Powder River country of Montana and Wyoming, "Where can I find your master?" The man replied, "He ain't been born yet!"[31]

That's it. No masters, not even a masterful state. This was the American achievement. But the economics of the Declaration were a decidedly mixed bag in cause, achievement, and outcome, in the short and long terms.

Notes

1. The 1789 population estimates are from University of Maryland, Baltimore County, "Slave, Free Black, and White Population, 1780–1830," https://userpages.umbc.edu/~bouton/History407/SlaveStats.htm. This source seems intelligently compiled. It uses data from the first federal census in 1790 to extrapolate back to 1789 the 7.8 percent of blacks who were not enslaved—and were among the considerable number of free blacks who fought on both sides in the Revolution.

2. Maya Jasanoff, *Liberty's Exiles: American Loyalists in the Revolutionary World* (New York: Random House, 2012), 357.

3. Jeremy Black, *Fighting for America: The Struggle for Mastery in North America, 1519–1871* (Bloomington, IN: Indiana University Press, 2011).

4. J. David Hacker, "A Census-Based Count of the Civil War Dead," *Civil War History* 57, no. 4 (December 2011): 307–48, https://muse.jhu.edu/article/465917.

5. David A. Blum and Nese F. DeBruyne, *American War and Military Operations Casualties: Lists and Statistics*, Congressional Research Service, July 29, 2020, https://fas.org/sgp/crs/natsec/RL32492.pdf.

6. Ben Baack, "Forging a Nation State: The Continental Congress and the Financing of the War of American Independence," *Economic History Review* 54, no. 4 (2001): 639–56, https://onlinelibrary.wiley.com/doi/10.1111/1468-0289.00206.

7. Baack, "Forging a Nation State."

8. Larry Sawers, "The Navigation Acts Revisited," *Economic History Review* 45, no. 2 (May 1992): 262–84, https://onlinelibrary.wiley.com/doi/abs/10.1111/j.1468-0289.1992.tb01301.x.

9. On this point, see Lawrence A. Harper, "Mercantilism and the American Revolution," *Canadian Historical Review* 23, no. 1 (March 1942): 1–15; Robert Paul Thomas, "A Quantitative Approach to the Study of the Effects of British Imperial Policy upon Colonial Welfare: Some Preliminary Findings," *Journal of Economic History* 25, no. 4 (1965): 615–38, https://www.cambridge.org/core/journals/journal-of-economic-history/article/abs/quantitative-approach-to-the-study-of-the-effects-of-british-imperial-policy-upon-colonial-welfare-some-preliminary-findings/1A0191715C8F10F1ED01E2894CF0E50F; and Gary M. Walton, "The New Economic History and the Burdens of the Navigation Acts," *Economic History Review* 24, no. 4 (November 1971): 533–42, https://onlinelibrary.wiley.com/doi/10.1111/j.1468-0289.1971.tb00192.x.

10. Gerald Gunderson, *A New Economic History of America* (New York: McGraw-Hill, 1976); and Joseph D. Reid Jr., "Economic Burden: Spark to the American Revolution?," *Journal of Economic History* 38, no. 1 (March 1978): 81–100, https://www.cambridge.org/core/journals/journal-of-economic-history/article/abs/economic-burden-spark-to-the-american-revolution/5D1EF4BF6F14CE036ED6E67DB1DBF6FF.

11. For notable examples, see Robert E. Brown, *Charles Beard and the Constitution: A Critical Analysis of "An Economic Interpretation of the Constitution"* (Princeton, NJ: Princeton University Press, 1956); and Bruce Ackerman, *We the People* (Cambridge, MA: Harvard University Press, 1991–98).

12. Robert A. McGuire, *To Form a More Perfect Union: A New Economic Interpretation of the United States Constitution* (New York: Oxford University Press, 2003).

13. Charles Sellers, *The Market Revolution: Jacksonian America, 1815–1846* (Oxford, UK: Oxford University Press, 1991). Charles Sellers used similar formulations in many writings.

14. William Blackstone, *Commentaries on the Laws of England*, 16th ed. (London: A. Strahan, 1825), 3:326.

15. Alice Hanson Jones, *Wealth of a Nation to Be: The American Colonies on the Eve of the Revolution* (New York: Columbia University Press, 1980).

16. Bernard Bailyn, "The Central Themes of the American Revolution: An Interpretation," in Stephen Kurtz and James Hutson, eds., *Essays on the American Revolution* (Chapel Hill, NC: University of North Carolina Press, 1973), 26–27.

17. Abigail Adams, letter to John Adams, March 31, 1776, Founders Online, https://founders.archives.gov/documents/Adams/04-01-02-0241.

18. Samuel Johnson, "Taxation No Tyranny. An Answer to the Resolutions and Address of the American Congress," Northern Illinois University Digital Library, April 4, 1775, https://digital.lib.niu.edu/islandora/object/niu-amarch%3A88769.

19. Adam Smith, *The Wealth of Nations* (New York: Modern Library, 2000), 651.

20. Mark O'Brien, *When Adam Delved and Eve Span: A History of the Peasants' Revolt* (London: Bookmarks, 2016).

21. Richard Rumbold et al., "The Last Words of Coll. Richard Rumbold, Mad. Alicia Lisle, Alderman Henry Cornish, and Mr. Richard Nelthrop Who Were Executed in England and Scotland for High Treason in the Year 1685," University of Michigan, https://name.umdl.umich.edu/A57890.0001.001. Thomas Jefferson paraphrased this line without attribution in his June 24, 1826, letter to the mayor of Washington, DC—the final letter he wrote—yet he did not liberate even by his last will and testament his enslaved people, as George Washington had. See Thomas Jefferson, letter to Roger Chew Weightman, June 24, 1826, Founders Online, https://founders.archives.gov/documents/Jefferson/98-01-02-6179. Thus in practice was the practical force of "all men created equal" among enlightened Virginians.

22. James C. Scott, *Seeing like a State: How Certain Schemes to Improve the Human Condition Have Failed* (New Haven, CT: Yale University Press, 2020); and James F. Searing, *West African Slavery and Atlantic Commerce: The Senegal River Valley, 1700–1860* (Cambridge, UK: Cambridge University Press, 2002), 407–29.

23. A similar effect was achieved in the northern German lands by the Zollverein in 1834 and by the German Empire in 1871. And the Austro-Hungarian Empire, though it had 11 official languages, was always a big free-trade zone internally. The US was externally a thoroughly protectionist country until the Kennedy Round of the 1960s, as were Austria, Germany, and Hungary on a similar timescale. But the claim, seeking to justify fresh protectionism, that protective tariffs in European countries and the US explain these countries' economic successes is mistaken. The internal markets were huge.

24. Peter H. Lindert and Jeffrey G. Williamson, *Unequal Gains: American Growth and Inequality Since 1700* (Princeton, NJ: Princeton University Press, 2016).

25. Jeffrey G. Williamson and Peter Lindert, "America's Revolution: Economic Disaster, Development, and Equality," Centre for Economic Policy Research, July 15, 2011, https://cepr.org/voxeu/columns/americas-revolution-economic-disaster-development-and-equality.

26. On this point, see Deirdre Nansen McCloskey, "How Growth Happens: Liberalism, Innovism, and the Great Enrichment" (working paper, Economic History Seminar, Northwestern University, Evanston, IL, November 29, 2018), https://www.deirdremccloskey.com/docs/pdf/McCloskey_HowGrowthHappens.pdf.

27. Alexis de Tocqueville, *Democracy in America*, trans. Harvey C. Mansfield and Delba Winthrop (Chicago: University of Chicago Press, 2000), 116.

28. Abraham Lincoln, "Lincoln's Second Inaugural Address" (speech, Washington, DC, March 4, 1865), https://www.nps.gov/linc/learn/historyculture/lincoln-second-inaugural.htm.

29. Benjamin Constant, "The Liberty of Ancients Compared with That of Moderns," Liberty Fund, 1819, https://oll.libertyfund.org/titles/constant-the-liberty-of-ancients-compared-with-that-of-moderns-1819.

30. Franklin D. Roosevelt, "1941 State of the Union Address 'The Four Freedoms,'" Voices of Democracy, January 6, 1941, https://voicesofdemocracy.umd.edu/fdr-the-four-freedoms-speech-text.

31. Oakley Hall, "Powder River Country: The Movies, the Wars, and the Teapot Dome," in Paul Andrew Hutton, ed., *Western Heritage: A Selection of Wrangler Award–Winning Articles* (Norman, OK: University of Oklahoma Press, 2011).

4

Laying the Foundations for a Market Economy

RICHARD A. EPSTEIN

The political separation pursued by the American founding was sharp and violent. But the transition to an independent American legal order was far less so. Note, for instance, the continuity between two systems in Article XXV of the 1777 New York Constitution:

> And this convention doth further, in the name and by the authority of the good people of this State, ordain, determine, and declare that such parts of the common law of England, and of the statute law of England and Great Britain, and of the acts of the legislature of the colony of New York, as together did form the law of the said colony on [April 19, 1777] shall be and continue the law of this State, subject to such alterations and provisions as the legislature of this State shall, from time to time, make concerning the same.[1]

Nor was this the only way in which the new regime derived from the old. The American constitutional system ultimately contained many features that were partial departures from the English model (like having a president and not a king). But much of its federal system was an adaptation that put the federal government in the place of the English government and left most of the governing to the states, deploying only (what seemed at the time) enumerated powers to define the federal government's role.

This relatively smooth doctrinal transition makes it possible to examine the American system in light of the English one. Unsurprisingly, many of the tensions evident in legal debates in Great Britain, which was in the midst of its first industrial revolution, carried over to the United States. This was especially true with what we would now call economic policy.

In the founding period (which for legal-history purposes we might say extends from 1776 to about 1835, with John Marshall's death), dealing with these issues was compounded by a set of conceptual obstacles that did not get resolved until the 19th century. Laissez-faire economics were at best in their infancy. The term "capitalism," with its largely negative connotations, also lay in the future.

The social welfare implications of competition versus monopoly were not yet worked out, so the defense of classical-liberal principles of limited government and strong property rights was captured largely in the term "commercial republic," which obviously understated the role that manufacturing, mining, and agriculture would play both during and after the founding period. It was therefore with a limited set of analytical tools that early Americans confronted many basic questions about the character of the commercial economy then emerging on both sides of the Atlantic.

At the heart of these tensions lay the constant struggle between protectionism and competition. And the nascent American political order addressed these tensions and that struggle in a complex way that would set the pattern for American economic debates ever since. That pattern is especially evident in the Constitution's structure and some early legal debates about its implementation.

The American Constitution was a charter in two major directions: Key structural provisions govern the relationship between the central government and the states on the one hand and between the divided powers in the federal government on the other. Further provisions gave protection to individual rights.

Most, but not all of these, were conducive to the market economy or capitalism as we now know it. But never in any simple way. And working out the place of markets, competition, and trade in the life of the new republic was a constant preoccupation of the courts in the nation's first half century. This is evident in a broad range of cases and controversies but can be illuminated by considering a few key domains in particular.

Free Trade Across Jurisdictional Boundaries

One of the effective preconditions of an exchange economy is that it allows for free trade between willing partners wherever they are located. Within a given jurisdiction, there are usually few, if any, territorial obstacles to free trade. But when trade crosses any jurisdictional boundaries, the government with power to exclude outsiders also has the power to exclude trade.

The Constitution took active steps to prevent the balkanization of trade within the United States and with it the weakening of the commercial republic by mercantilist policies of the sort that Adam Smith so roundly attacked in the *Wealth of Nations*. Thus, Article I, Section 10 prohibits any state, without Congress's consent, from imposing a tax on any import or export, except as is "absolutely necessary" to run local inspection laws intended to prevent the movement of dangerous goods from foreign nations.[2]

In *Brown v. Maryland* (1827), Chief Justice Marshall rejected a Maryland scheme that did not impose such a tax on the imports but only on the importer when the goods in question exceeded $50 in value (a bit over $1,000 today). The chief justice stressed that the clause's purpose was to encourage harmony within the United States and with foreign nations.

His interpretation prevented a circumvention of the Constitution by shifting the tax from the good to the person: "There is no difference, in effect, between a power to prohibit the sale of an article and a power to prohibit its introduction into the country."[3] He then developed an "original packet" doctrine to set the time at which the goods were no longer insulated from local taxation, by being mixed in with other goods within a given state.

By way of analogy, the later decision in *Almy v. California* held that the import-export prohibitions were applicable to transactions between two states, where the same free trade spirit animated.[4] A similar free trade spirit is behind the provision in Article I, Section 9, which states categorically that "no Tax or Duty shall be laid on Articles exported from any State." This clause in fact eliminates a powerful impediment to free trade, given that the imposition of such taxes would slow down commerce and perhaps confer a competitive advantage to some states over others.[5]

Taxes of this sort provoke far less opposition than tariffs on foreign imports, such as those Hamilton defended as a protection for infant industries. Hence, in *Federalist* 11, Hamilton made clear that Congress had the power to reject, as it were, Smith's teachings on this point. It is worth noting the tariff on key imports created one of the wedge issues that led to the Civil War, as Southerners bristled against taxes on imports that gave Northerners a key advantage by increasing the price of foreign goods destined for Southern ports.

Closely related to the import-export clause is the general statement of the commerce clause, which reads: "Congress shall have the power to . . . regulate commerce with foreign nations, among the several states and with the Indian tribes."[6] The early discussions of the clause concentrated on trade with foreign nations, in which the dominant sense, gleaned as well from *Federalist* 11, was not supportive of freedom of foreign trade to cross into our national borders.[7]

To the contrary, the foreign commerce clause allowed Congress to impose tariffs and other regulations in ways that aligned with Hamilton's mercantilist sentiments. The domestic use of the clause delivers a more mixed message: domestic free trade behind a tariff wall. One problem was that states could not have the power to stop the movement of goods and services across state lines, so the question was how the federal government's power to regulate commerce either advanced or retarded trade.

In practice, both effects seemed to matter. On this front, the great case of the founding period was *Gibbons v. Ogden* (1824).[8] Aaron Ogden, an assignee of Robert Fulton, the inventor of the steamboat, had received under New York law an exclusive license to operate steamboats in New York state waters in exchange for developing the new steam technology. Thomas Gibbons wished to operate a steamboat from Elizabethtown, New Jersey, into New York City, but New York courts honored the exclusive grant, which Gibbons then attacked in federal courts.

In the Supreme Court, Chief Justice Marshall overrode the New York state courts and held that, as a constitutional matter, regulating commerce was not limited to regulating border crossings but covered all navigation that went from the interior of one state to the interior of another.[9] This meant that Ogden could not exclude him from the state, a boost for free navigation. But the same decision held that the United States could itself regulate the entire matter by issuing coastal licenses to various vessels, which could allow it to block that coastal trade. So the clause had a dual effect, first by limiting state monopoly power but then by encouraging federal monopoly power.

This argument thus gives rise to a serious theoretical problem: Could Congress, under the guise of "encouraging and protecting domestic manufacturers," pass a law that prohibited Southern imports into another state by keeping them out of the stream of commerce? To allow that would let the federal government choke off interstate commerce from slave states, which easily could have toppled the Union. Justice Joseph Story was firmly against this, and when, in 1918, the same issue came up with the shipment of goods made with underaged child labor, a narrow 5–4 Supreme Court majority struck the effort down on the grounds that this use of federal monopoly power (although they did not use those words) upended the original division of power between the state and federal government, which had been far more acute a century before.[10]

Further complications also stemmed from *Gibbons* proper. In a concurring opinion, Justice William Johnson held that federal dominance of navigation between states could be asserted even if the federal government had passed no law at all. This gave rise to the question of what, if anything, states could do to interfere with federal power dealing with local systems of health and safety.

Shortly thereafter, *Willson v. Black-Bird Creek Marsh Co.* held that the state could construct a dam across a navigable waterway even if it interfered with navigation with interstate commerce that passed through the state.[11] But the state had a strong police power justification that its measures improved the health of the population.

The assertion of this legitimate interest controlled the outcome, but for Marshall the result would have been different if the federal government had passed legislation pursuant to the commerce clause to govern these navigable rivers. As it did not, the conflict was avoided, because the Johnson theory was not accepted. Down the road, some trade-off would have to be made when the two interests collided.

The parallel issue concerned the import-export clause. When does the federal power end and the state power begin? In *New York v. Miln*, the Court, just after the close of the Marshall era, upheld New York's inspection law for goods entering the state.[12] This offered a sensible accommodation between the federal interest in navigation and the state's internal police power.

This interplay been state and federal interests in commerce has continued into modern times, when an odd but durable synthesis has developed. Once the issue of slavery was off the table, the affirmative power of commerce steadily expanded. It first covered local transportation in competition with interstate transaction in the Shreveport Rate Cases,[13] expanding to all transportation, whether state or federal, as part of the railroad grid in *Railroad Commission of Wisconsin v. Chicago, Burlington & Quincy R. R. Co.*[14]

Finally, the clause reached all activities of any type that embraced manufacturng, agriculture, and mining as part of national commerce, permitting the federal government the power to organize monopoly pricing across multiple markets, including agriculture, motor vehicles, and labor. Thus, any serious limitations on the scope of what Congress could enact were effectively scotched.[15]

But at the same time, the anticompetitive impulses were given their strongest expressions by preventing any state from engaging in any form of discrimination between domestic and foreign rates to create a level platform for interstate competition.[16] Both forms of regulation deviate from competitive norms. But various states blocking interstate competition more clearly disrupts trade than the price increases associated with various kinds of marketing orders. Decisions made in the founding period clearly influenced future outcomes but did not dictate them.

Takings and Procedural Due Process

The stress on the commercial society also misses another precondition for the successful emergence of a capitalist system: the protection of property from confiscation. This development started in England with the acceptance of two provisions of the Magna Carta:

> (39) No free man shall be seized or imprisoned, or stripped of his rights or possessions, or outlawed or exiled, or deprived of his standing in any other way, nor will we proceed with force against him, or send others to do so, except by the lawful judgement of his equals or by the law of the land.
> (40) To no one will we sell, to no one deny or delay right or justice.[17]

These two provisions worked to prevent the Crown's arbitrary seizure of property in all its forms. They functioned to eliminate any situation in which judges of the Crown would play favorites among its various subjects. No system of capitalism could possibly work without these protections. In the founding period, these principles were expressed in the Constitution by the combined operation of two provisions of the Fifth Amendment: "Nor [shall any person] be deprived of life, liberty, or property, without due process of law; nor shall private property be taken for public use, without just compensation."[18] These provisions did not receive their authoritative expositions during the founding period, but only long afterward.

Thus, the due process clause received its first reading in 1884 in *Hurtado v. California*, which held that presentment before a grand jury was not part of that basic protection, so it was possible to proceed by the less formal process of information.[19] On this view, due process, which covered chiefly the two great natural law principles of hearing the other side (*audi alteram partem*) and protection against a biased tribunal (*nemo judex in causa sua*), were of great applicability and purpose. Their unquestioned acceptance during the founding period did much to secure the future developments of the modern capitalist economy by introducing a strong rule-of-law component into the system at its formative stages, although this was compromised by the administrative reforms of the Progressive and New Deal eras, which tended to prefer the expertise of the administrative state to the decentralized activities of a competitive market.[20]

And on the takings side of the agenda, the most notable case of the founding period was *Barron v. Baltimore*, which raised the peculiar question of whether actions by the local government that denied John Barron access to a deepwater port counted as a taking for which redress was possible under federal law in a suit that the property owner had initiated in state court.[21]

Chief Justice Marshall did not address the substantive question, which gave rise to extensive litigation in subsequent years. No one obtained a federal remedy until 1897, over 30 years after the Civil War, when the adoption of a due process clause against the states in the 14th Amendment was held to trigger a federal response (in that instance, in a ratemaking case for railroads that had no factual parallel during the founding period, according to Justice John Marshall Harlan).[22] But, as a matter of constitutional interpretation, Marshall also held (relying on the passive voice in the Fifth Amendment—"nor shall private property be taken") that the protection of the takings clause applied to only the federal government and not the states.

States, for the most part, had adopted similar clauses into their own constitutions, but state takings were subject to enforcement and interpretation by state courts, which tended to work in parallel to the federal government. More specifically, the power of the natural law tradition in the founding period was strong, including perhaps the most notable decision of Chancellor James Kent in *Gardner v. Village of Newburgh* (1816).[23] Kent, resolving a dispute that arose from an improper diversion of water rights, held that it did not matter that the New York Constitution contained no explicit protection against takings. Rather, takings without compensation could be barred on natural law grounds:

> A right to a stream of water is as sacred as a right to the soil over which it flows. It is a part of the freehold, of which no man can be disseised "but by lawful judgment of his peers, or by due process of law." This is an ancient and fundamental maxim of common right to be found in *Magna Charta*, and which the legislature has incorporated into an act declaratory of the rights of the citizens of this state.[24]

The protection of patents and copyrights in the Constitution points in the same direction. The success of a federalist system depends on the effective protection of rights by both state and national governments, which was the norm throughout this period, so that no disjunction on the protection of basic rights existed anywhere throughout the system.

The Right to Contract

The Constitution's basic structure did not offer any generalized protection of the commercial economy insofar as it involved the freedom to make binding contracts free from interference either by the state or the national government. So once again (as with the future use of the takings clause), the contracts clause that on its face was applicable only to the states—where most regulatory activities took place—had an outsized career that started in the founding period but carried through to the Civil War. The clause reads: "No State shall . . . pass any Bill of Attainder, ex post facto Law, or Law impairing the Obligation of Contracts, or grant any Title of Nobility."[25]

The question is: How far does this clause go to protect the legal structure of property rights under the general classical-liberal system? To answer that question, it is necessary to break out the two separate branches of case law articulated in the founding period.

The first applies to contracts between two (or more) *private* parties. To what extent does the contracts clause protect against state interference, and to what extent is the protection so provided consistent with classical-liberal principles? The second question, which is not quite apparent from the constitutional text, is to what extent the contracts clause protects private parties that have entered into agreements or obtained *public* charters from the state against actions that impair these obligations.

To begin, it's worth noting the odd contours of the clause, which left its scope uncertain during the founding period. As drafted, the clause binds only the states and therefore does not afford any protection against the federal government. But no accessible theory explains why that protection extends to only one level of interference—the state—when the same perils of market disruption can arise from federal interference with contracts.

Yet parallel protections against both the state and federal government are found with the bills of attainder, prohibited to the United States and the states. The same is true of ex post facto laws that are blocked to both the federal government and the states. The obvious explanation is that both levels of government are susceptible to the abuse, which was all too well established in English practice. Government disrespect for contracts is always possible at both levels of government; yet ironically, it appears that the contracts clause was designed in part to protect contracts between individuals from two or more states, which is perfectly consistent with its broad language.

Initially, the clause was intended to stop the spate of state debtor relief laws that either eliminated or reduced the amounts owing on a variety of contracts, which if allowed could destabilize the entire system of credit.[26]

But the text of the clause reads more broadly, for the clause contains no explicit subject matter limitation. Yet as noted, no obvious link connects this clause to some distinct federalism issue, such as the use of negotiable instruments across state lines.[27]

In addition, the peculiar phrasing of the guarantee, which talks about the "Obligation of Contracts," plural, raises the question of what counts as an obligation. Everyone agrees that it covers the obligation of the party to pay or perform. However, it is a closer question whether the clause imposes obligations on the creditor. This would, for example, prevent the creditor from suing to collect the debt before it is due or before some condition precedent to payment has been satisfied. Additionally, it could affect cases in which the legislature revives litigation after the statute of limitations has expired or blocks a cause of action before the time allowed under the statute.[28]

A system that tries to ensure stability and integrity should in principle bind both parties in all these situations to advance the classical-liberal ideal of the complete protection of the contractual arrangement. Indeed, the most important definition of contract at the time was that of Frenchman Robert Joseph Pothier, who wrote in broad natural law terms that a contract is "an agreement by which two parties reciprocally promise and engage or one of them singly promises to the other to give some particular thing, or to do or abstain from doing some particular act."[29]

In the civil law systems, this covered not only bargains and exchanges but also unilateral actions, including the release of a debt or other obligation, without consideration of some prior obligations. Pothier died in 1772, but after the ratification of the US Constitution, Chief Justice Marshall echoed that theme when he wrote that "a contract is an agreement in which a party undertakes to do or not to do a particular thing."[30] So it appears that the scope of the clause is broad in all these cases. The question then is how it applies in concrete cases.

On this score, the question of debtor's relief again comes to the fore, because the question is whether the contracts clause in its absolutist terms prohibits adjustment of creditors' rights through some kind of bankruptcy protection. This was a crucial question, given that Article I, Section 8 of the Constitution stipulates that Congress can establish "uniform Laws on the subject of Bankruptcies throughout the United States," without vesting all the powers over these bankruptcies exclusively in the federal government.

In *Sturges v. Crowninshield*, the Supreme Court let the states enact their own insolvency laws—decentralized processes without a centralized court in which claims can be processed or the business reorganized—unless they required an impairment of contract or were superseded by a federal bankruptcy act.[31] The second issue was not in question here because there was no federal statute. The first issue, however, was in play. The Supreme Court, after much anxiety, applied the protection of the contracts clause to the creditor, even though the debtor was required to surrender all his property to obtain the needed protection. As a general matter, the chief justice took

> the distinction between the obligation of a contract and the remedy given by the legislature to enforce that obligation has been taken at the bar and exists in the nature of things. Without impairing the obligation of the contract, the remedy may certainly be modified as the wisdom of the nation shall direct.[32]

He then concluded that in this case, the New York law "so far as it attempts to discharge this defendant from the debt in the declaration mentioned, is contrary to the Constitution of the United States, and that the plea is no bar to the action."[33]

There is an obvious tension between the state's ability to modify a remedy and the state's ability to end the obligation altogether, which is not solved by alluding to "the nature of things." But why and how this should work was not clear, because Chief Justice Marshall had no accurate conception of the proper function of either a state insolvency law or a federal bankruptcy law. An explanation as to why the release should be allowed in whole or in part was needed.

On this point, Marshall missed the best explanation: The restriction of the remedy should be allowed whenever other adjustments in these credit arrangements can increase the deal's overall value. This could be achieved by offering the creditor a form of quid pro quo that counts as just compensation for barring their direct suit.[34]

As drafted, the contracts clause does not contain any reference to just compensation, but the correct argument should be that if the rearrangement secures the orderly reassignment of assets in ways that better all parties, it should be allowed. On the topic of state contracts, to which I shall turn shortly, *West River Bridge Co. v. Dix* did not cite *Gardner*, but it did allude to the same principle of natural law that it held was incorporated into all contracts:

> There enter conditions which arise not out of the literal terms of the contract itself; they are superinduced by the preexisting and higher authority of the laws of nature, of nations, or of the community to which the parties belong; . . . Every contract is made in subordination to them, and must yield to their control, as conditions inherent and paramount, wherever a necessity for their execution shall occur. Such a condition is the right of eminent domain.[35]

This formula reads a just compensation component into the clause. How does that arise? If these obligations are fully shielded from bankruptcy, all creditors will race to court to collect their debts, which could easily force the early collapse of the debtor's business, leaving less to go around for all creditors.

Either a state insolvency law or a federal bankruptcy should be allowed to block this result by stopping contractual enforcement so long as the assets are collected and managed collectively to produce the desired result. Thus, with this expanded perspective, the procedure should be allowed to go forward so long as the new arrangement contains protections against illegal diversions and favoritism, as all bankruptcy and insolvency laws do.

These issues were left untouched until the great case of *Ogden v. Saunders*, in which the Court held, 4–3 with both Marshall and Story in dissent, that a bankruptcy law passed *after* the creation of the obligation could block the enforcement of the obligation.[36] Justice Bushrod Washington said that the discharge had to be allowed, for otherwise the statute of frauds (which renders unenforceable certain unsigned contracts) would also count as an impairment of contract. He thought that result was indefensible since the statute was hailed as one of the great legal reforms after its initial adoption in England in 1677.[37] The same conclusion held as well for statutes of limitation, which likewise had from time immemorial cut off stale causes of action.

In dissent, Chief Justice Marshall noted the distinction between this case and *Sturges*: "In *Sturges v. Crowninshield*, the law acted on a contract which was made before its passage; in this case, the contract was entered into after the passage of the law."[38] Hence in the former case, the creditor had no notice of the law and thus could not protect himself against its application. Here the law was passed first, so the parties had ample time to adjust.

Clearly that difference means that the second statute, if it impairs the contract, does so less intrusively than the former. But for Chief Justice Marshall, the distinction did not stick. Indeed, he could not mount an effective response to claims that his view would undermine the statute of frauds, statutes of limitation, and usury laws.

But by the same token, he had a challenge that the majority could not answer. Suppose a state legislature passed a law saying that all contracts formed after this date may be modified thereafter at the legislature's will. The constitutional guarantee then becomes empty if a simple statute can override it.

How best to fix this difficulty? At this point, recall that the rigid rule in *Sturges* was untenable because, the Constitution to one side, no social justification should prevent the needed adjustments when major condition precedents failed. So even though this contract was put into effect before the statute was passed, the correct question to ask was in principle whether, in *Sturges*, the law at the time it was passed provided some system-wide social benefit.

That same analysis works here. There is not an absolute, but only prima facie, obligation not to impair contracts. But the just compensation referred to in *Dix* carries over to private contracts as well. The same is true of the statutes of limitations that generally improve the operation of the legal system by weeding out stale claims that are difficult to prove or deny. These claims typically are not barred but will generally be pursued earlier with greater reliability and smaller expense. That improvement is shared generally so that just compensation is implicit in these cases, even as it presumptively impairs the contracts of all.

The same principle applies as well to the security of transactions increased by a recordation statute, which subordinates a valid unrecorded conveyance to a subsequent one that was recorded first. Surely, the first contract is impaired because its subordination deviates from the prior-in-time, higher-in-right rule that has been a staple of the private law since Roman times.[39] And after a fashion, a contract can be impaired by a change in the parol evidence rules that alters what kind of evidence can be introduced into case. "Big deal" is the right response, given that neither side knows who will be hurt or helped down the road. If the law seems to make a general improvement, it should prevail.

Under these examples, the just compensation principle avoids the incorrect rigidity of a hard libertarian rule that says all promises must be enforced—period—and a wholly formless situation in which any trans-formation of basic obligations is good so long as the legislature decrees it. Indeed, therein lies the key mistake of Justice Washington's opinion: He draws no distinction between statutes of limitations and statutes of fraud on the one side and usury laws on the other. The logic of implicit-in-kind compensation, however, cannot save usury laws that apply to discrete classes of lenders by imposing undue restraints on vital financial markets, without offering any compensation to the losers in these rigged markets. Hence, they are naked wealth transfers of the sort that any classical-liberal constitutional theory condemns.

That same argument can be made about *selective* exceptions to either statutes of frauds or statutes of limitations that skew to a favored class of individuals. At this point, there is a taking from A to B that is imposed without compensation, and that transfer looks like a form of disguised theft because there is no justification (like the prevention of force and fraud under the police power) to deal with the situation. In the founding period, political forces kept these divisive forces in check, and the basic framework held through thick and thin into the 1930s.[40] But the seeds of the future maneuvers were laid by the weak conceptual foundations when *both* sides missed the sensible legal ground that develops from the classical-liberal theory that animates the best of what is in the founders' Constitution.

The second half of any historical reading of the contracts clause deals with its application to public bodies. From the outset, no other all-purpose provision of the Constitution applied to commercial transactions generally, as any use of the takings clause lay in the future. Yet the general classical-liberal theory of limited government does not allow the state to make whatever deal it desired. That limitation of state power in *Gibbons* should have constrained the creation of any exclusive franchise to Fulton to operate steamboats in New York waters, given that the state received nothing in return from Fulton, who independently had patent protection for developing the steamship and thus should not have received that additional spur.

However, many transactions revealed serious irregularities by state legislatures. The first of these was *Fletcher v. Peck*.[41] That case arose out of the Yazoo land scandal of 1795 involving huge tracts of land that Georgia's legislature sold to land speculators at ridiculously low prices, even as native tribes claimed sovereignty over those same lands. Shortly after the sales, it was discovered that many Georgia legislators had been bribed.

Accordingly, Georgia's legislature in January 1795 passed a statute that purported to reverse the sales, given that obvious fraud. But after it reversed the grants, John Peck, a Massachusetts speculator, resold 15,000 acres of land for $3,000 to Robert Fletcher. When Peck refused to deliver, Fletcher sued him in what was widely understood to be a collusive transaction to secure all the speculators' titles.

Amazingly, this thoroughly corrupt bargain was upheld, for both good and bad reasons. The good part of the decision was that the Court, speaking through Chief Justice Marshall, held that the contracts clause covered grants made by the government to private parties, which is strictly necessary if there were to be any federal constraint on abuses by state legislatures whose courts might or might not be responsive to the danger. But the bad part of *Fletcher* was how Marshall mangled the analysis of the transaction by showing the same rigidity toward contractual obligations that marred his later decision in *Sturges.*

Marshall claimed that no court could inquire into the legislature's motives because its obligation was absolute under some jumbled combination of natural and statutory law. That contention was just false. As noted earlier, the principles of trust law (which impose extensive good-faith duties) applied equally to public and private transactions.[42] Thus, if this transaction had been a grant by the officers or directors of a private corporation that was tainted by fraud, it could surely be set aside so long as the original recipient possessed the property received direct from the state.

The difficulties arise (as in the case of bills of exchange) where the property (like the bill) was transferred by the fraudulent recipient to a third party. If that party received in good faith—for example, without knowledge of the fraud—the original transferor (here Georgia) could have a damage action against only the original buyer. But this transaction was collusive, as both Peck and Fletcher wanted to insulate all sales from judicial scrutiny, which Marshall's opinion did.

At this point, any inquiry into motive would have exposed all the parties as acting in bad faith and set aside the transactions, which would have done much to rehabilitate the tribal claims to the land. So once again, classical-liberal principles received at most a partial vindication.

It was the positive portion of *Fletcher* that lived on in *Dartmouth College v. Woodward,* when the New Hampshire legislature gutted the initial 1769 royal charter that organized the college as a private institution.[43] The 1816 New Hampshire legislation transferred effective control of the college to the governor, done in the short run to reinstate a deposed president.

That kind of usurpation can be discovered only by looking at the records and purpose of the transaction, at which point it was an open-and-shut case of usurpation that the Marshall opinion stopped in its tracks, with only two cursory references to *Fletcher*, both to the effect that charters were contracts. The transaction struck down in *Dartmouth College* was a masterpiece of circumvention, and today the elaborate body of fraudulent conveyance and public trust doctrine has undone the worst of *Fletcher*. Its legacy lives on mostly as a constructive protection of the commercial economy and its ideals.

Patents and Copyrights

The protection of property rights during the founding period was encapsulated most clearly in Article I, Section 8, Clause 8, which provides that "the Congress shall have power . . . To promote the Progress of Science and useful Arts, by securing for limited Times to Authors and Inventors the exclusive Right to their respective Writings and Discoveries."[44]

There is a great deal that is packed into the clause, whose strength comes from the interlocking impact of two complementary theories. On the one hand, much influenced by Lockean theory, a patent is treated as a form of property awarded as a recognition of the labor that an inventor or author has put into creating their work. On the other, that labor is protected because it creates an incentive for work that benefits society as a whole.

Thus, Section 1 of the Patent Act of 1790 states "that he, she, or they, hath or have invented or discovered any useful art, manufacture, engine, machine, or device, or any improvement therein not before known or used, and praying that a patent may be granted therefor."[45] I have long argued that these two overlapping justifications are complementary,[46] and an excellent detailed history of the early republican period written by

Adam Mossoff shows how these dual themes played out in not only the United States but also England and the continent.[47]

Now look more closely at their constitutional protection. The power to protect patents and copyrights is conferred on the federal government so that there is no need to negotiate multiple different patent and copyright regimes at the state level. Uniformity here is a value, partly because of the sharp reduction in the cost of organizing a registry of some sort to keep track of who owns what. There is no "natural" right to property here, that a person can protect by taking possession of some material thing, if other persons are allowed to fabricate an invention or reproduce the writing of another person. And although Congress had no obligation to protect these forms of right, the practical pressures were so strong that it enacted the Patent Act of 1790 and the Copyright Act of 1790, both of which contain many critical features that still organize these areas of law today.

First, the precatory clause, "To promote the Progress of Science and useful Arts," does not just refer to the notion of utilitarian advancement.[48] It also signals that the government could only issue patents and copyrights for these limited purposes, which thus ruled out their use to allow importers and local officials to secure monopoly control over certain markets. This provision is a huge victory for the classical-liberal perspective on this issue, which means that the federal government could not create the types of monopolies in other areas that should have been, and often were, stopped by an application of the public trust doctrine.

The last phrase, "By securing for limited Times to Authors and Inventors the exclusive Right to their respective Writings and Discoveries," also helps design a sensible system. These rights are granted only for limited times and thus are held in contrast to the perpetual ownership over land or chattels, which is the hallmark of an efficient system of property rights in tangibles. The "long term" means that the owner of land or chattels does not have to puzzle as to what will be done with their house or furniture when some (arbitrary) initial period of ownership expires. It does no good to cast them out into the world and none to allow other individuals to seize them.

The perpetual time horizon allows individuals to develop and improve property without any fear that others will wrest it away from them. Thus, when the owner leases out property for some limited term, the party can make arrangements with the lessee as to what will be done with any improvement at the termination of the lease, so as to avoid that free-for-all.

Nonetheless, copyrights and patents present a fundamentally different trade-off from other forms of property. At any time after the specification of an invention or the preparation of a copyrightable work, anyone could produce their own object or writing without the cooperation of their owner, and at low cost. So if the only issue on the table is the maximum output conditional on the prior invention of the object or writing, the only protection that should be given to the inventor or author is of the particular objects that they produce. But that caveat is key. Few individuals will make any invention or writing for public use at some private cost to themselves if others are entitled to produce the same ultimate good without having to incur the costs of its creation.

Thus, without the exclusive right, many inventions would not be made or distributed to the broader public. The exclusive right usefully changes the social equation, for now there is a sufficiently long time to recoup the initial invention or writing where the creator has an exclusive right—which was the exact strategy that was used when the government gave a company the exclusive right to build a bridge: rights to charge for a period to recover costs and then a sharp or complete reduction in fees.[49] But that right is for only a limited term—14 years for a copyright, with renewal, and 14 years for a patent—because its perpetual protection will prevent others from entering that market at any future time.

Hence the law recognizes a trade-off by putting things into the public domain where they can be used by anyone against not only the original creator but also anyone else who has an exclusive right in another invention or writing that is put up for sale. So, it is wrong to think that a patent creates a monopoly when other inventors or writers face competition from other parties with substitute patented technologies. At this point, an important distinction emerges.

It is usually easy enough to figure out who has copied whose novel or poem, so that registration is freely given and any disputes over infringement or originality can take place ex post facto. But it is hard to know the exact scope of a patent. From the earliest time, a system of ex ante examination is designed to make an initial determination of patent validity. This process requires identifying "any new and useful process, machine, manufacture, or composition of matter." It also necessitates demonstrating that the advance is significant enough to merit the protection of the patent law. Further, disclosures about the modes of production must be made so that the rest of the world can gain knowledge.[50]

Care was also taken to see that matters that belonged in the public domain—natural substances and mathematical formulas—could not be taken private. Copyright had less demanding requirements for originality, but here, too, care had to be taken to make sure that matters that were already in the public domain could not be removed. The work done here was quite impressive, and much of it was shepherded through the courts by Justice and Professor Story, a formidable figure in the field until his death in 1845. The initial period thus laid a firm foundation for further work in the area. The principles articulated then still govern today.

The Pillars of a Market Economy

Each of these complicated issues and a number of others (such as the national bank and common carriers) were addressed by legislators and judges in the founding era. Each then became the basis of case law throughout the 19th century, whether in taking up commercial transactions, due process, property rights, the public trust doctrine, or the scope of federal power under the commerce clause. And each remains a crucial foundation of the law underlying the American commercial republic in our time.

In the founding period, there was a tussle between principles of economic protectionism and monopoly power on the one hand and free trade and competition on the other. Struggles this deep and fundamental never yield black-and-white answers, but rather shift back and forth within and across different historical periods. On balance, the legislators and judges of the founding period had more sound than unsound classical-liberal instincts and thus charted a course that gave the initial edge to the desirable attributes of a sound capitalist, or free-market, system. But the character of that system has always been in question.

When Benjamin Franklin was asked what kind of Constitution the 1787 convention had created, he is said to have responded, "A republic, if you can keep it." If we consider what kind of economic system the American republic has sought to make possible, the answer suggested by the constitutional thought and practice of the founding era might be similar: "a market system, if you can keep it."

Notes

1. N.Y. Const. of 1777.
2. US Const. art. I, § 10.
3. *Brown v. Maryland*, 25 US 419, 439 (1827).
4. *Almy v. California*, 65 US 169 (1860).
5. US Const. art. I, § 9, cl. 5.
6. US Const. art. I, § 8, cl. 3. See Robert G. Natelson, "The Meaning of 'Regulate Commerce' to the Constitution's Ratifiers," *Federalist Society Review* 21 (2022): 308. For a contemporary exposition, see Joseph Story, *Commentaries on the Constitution of the United States*, ed. Ronald D. Rotunda and John E. Nowak (1833; Durham, NC: Carolina Academic Press, 1987). The sections on the commerce clause are §§ 510–35, which closely follow the views of Chief Justice John Marshall, to whom Joseph Story dedicated the volume. The juxtaposition of foreign, domestic, and Indian commerce suggests that all relate to activities across state lines. Their histories have wildly varied. For a broader perspective, see Jack M. Balkin, "Commerce," *Michigan Law Review* 109 (2010): 1. For my views, see Richard A. Epstein, "The Proper Scope of the Commerce Power," *Virginia Law Review* 73 (1987): 1387. Story offers strong support for Natelson's position.
7. See *Federalist*, no. 11 (Alexander Hamilton). This takes the position that we should advance "Active Commerce in our own bottoms." And further: "If we continue united, we may counteract a policy so unfriendly to our prosperity in a variety of ways. By prohibitory regulations, extending at the same time throughout the States,

we may oblige foreign countries to bid against each other, for the privileges of our markets. This assertion will not appear chimerical to those who are able to appreciate the importance." All this is a dangerous game that hurts consumers on the one side and, critically, potential exporters who need cheap imports to lower their cost of making sales overseas.

8. *Gibbons v. Ogden*, 22 US 1 (1824).

9. *Livingston v. Van Ingen*, 9 Johns. R. 507 (N.Y. 1812), written by Chancellor James Kent, a major figure of the period, the first professor at Columbia University Law School, and the author of *Commentaries on American Law*.

10. *Hammer v. Dagenhart*, 247 US 251 (1918).

11. *Willson v. Black-Bird Creek Marsh Co.*, 27 US 245 (1829).

12. *New York v. Miln*, 36 US 102 (1837).

13. *Houston East and West Texas Railway Co. v. United States*, 234 US 342 (1914).

14. See *Railroad Commission of Wisconsin v. Chicago, Burlington & Quincy R. R. Co.*, 257 US 563 (1921) (allowing the regulation of intrastate rates given that the property is used in both domestic and interstate commerce).

15. For the most dramatic case, see *Wickard v. Filburn*, 312 US 111 (1942) (allowing the price regulation of grain fed to one's own cows).

16. *H. P. Hood & Sons v. Du Mond*, 336 US 525 (1949); and *Dean Milk Co. v. City of Madison*, 340 US 349 (1951).

17. Magna Carta (1215).

18. US Const. amend. V.

19. *Hurtado v. California*, 110 US 516 (1884).

20. See Woodrow Wilson, *Congressional Government: A Study in American Politics* (Riverside Press, 1885); and James Landis, *The Administrative Process* (New Haven, CT: Yale University Press, 1938). For my overview, see Richard A. Epstein, *Design for Liberty: Private Property, Public Administration, and the Rule of Law* (Cambridge, MA: Harvard University Press, 2011).

21. *Barron v. Baltimore*, 32 US 233 (1833).

22. *Chicago, Quincy & Burlington Railroad Co. v. Chicago*, 166 US 226 (1897).

23. *Gardner v. Village of Newburgh*, 2 Johns. Ch. 162 (N.Y. 1816). *Gardner* was the "most prominent" of these cases but by no means the only one. See James W. Ely, "The Oxymoron Reconsidered: Myth and Reality in the Origins of Substantive Due Process," *Constitutional Commentary* 16, no. 315 (1999): 334.

24. *Gardner*, 2 Johns. at 164, 166.

25. US Const. art. I, § 10, cl. 1. See *Federalist*, no. 44 (James Madison) (dealing with the clause). For general accounts, see Benjamin Fletcher Wright Jr., *The Contract Clause of the Constitution* (Cambridge, MA: Harvard University Press, 1938), 3–26; and Robert L. Hale, "The Supreme Court and the Contract Clause (Pts. 1–3)," *Harvard Law Review* 57, no. 512 (1944): 621, 852. For my views, see Richard A. Epstein, "Toward a Revitalization of the Contracts Clause," *University of Chicago Law Review* 51 (1984): 703.

26. *Federalist*, no. 10 (James Madison).

27. *Swift v. Tyson*, 41 US 1 (1842) (for the defense of this result in the Supreme Court). Chancellor Kent had taken the same position as a matter of state law. See James Kent, *Commentaries on American Law* (Claitor's Pub Division, 1826), 3:81, cited in *Swift*, 41 US at 17.

28. *Sturges v. Crowninshield*, 17 US 122, 207 (1819) ("If, in a state where six years may be pleaded in bar to an action of assumpsit, a law should pass declaring that contracts already in existence, not barred by the statute, should be construed to be within it, there could be little doubt of its unconstitutionality").

29. Robert Joseph Pothier, *A Treatise on the Law of Obligations or Contracts*, trans. William David Evans (Lawbook Exchange, 1853), 1:105.

30. *Sturges*, 17 US at 197.

31. *Sturges*, 17 US at 197.

32. *Sturges*, 17 US at 200.

33. *Sturges*, 17 US at 208.

34. This is the central theme. See Epstein, "Toward a Revitalization of the Contracts Clause," 703, 740–47; and Richard A. Epstein, *Takings: Private Property and the Power of Eminent Domain*, pt. 4 (Cambridge, MA: Harvard University Press, 1985) (showing how the same dynamic works in takings cases).

35. *West River Bridge Co. v. Dix*, 47 US 507, 532–34 (1848).

36. *Ogden v. Saunders*, 25 US 213 (1827).

37. Douglas Stollery, "Statute of Frauds," *Alberta Law Review* 14 (1976): 222–23.

38. *Ogden*, 25 US at 215.

39. In *Jackson v. Lamphire*, 28 US (3 Pet.) 280, 289 (1830), the Court upheld the state's power to enact a recordation system notwithstanding the contract clause. The result in the case is correct, but the opinion itself is only a collection of platitudes.

40. For something like the end, see *Home Building and Loan Association v. Blaisdell*, 290 US 398 (1934).

41. *Fletcher v. Peck*, 10 US 87 (1810). For a concise account of the case, see Federal Judicial Center, "*Fletcher v. Peck* (1810)," https://www.fjc.gov/history/cases/cases-that-shaped-the-federal-courts/fletcher-v-peck. Story argued to uphold the validity of the contract the year before he was elevated to the bench.

42. See Natelson, "The Meaning of 'Regulate Commerce' to the Constitution's Ratifiers."

43. *Dartmouth College v. Woodward*, 17 US 518 (1819).

44. US Const. art. I, § 8, cl. 3.

45. Patent Act of 1790, 1 Stat. 109, § 1.

46. Richard A. Epstein, "The Utilitarian Foundations of Natural Law," *Harvard Journal of Law & Public Policy* 12 (1989): 713.

47. Adam Mossoff, "Rethinking the Development of Patents: An Intellectual History, 1550–1800," *Hastings Law Journal* 52 (2001): 1255.

48. Patent Act of 1790, 1 Stat. 109, § 1.

49. *Charles River Bridge v. Warren Bridge*, 36 US 420 (1837). This case ended in a 4–3 split in which the grant was not held exclusive, which is why the Warren Bridge was cheek by jowl next to the Charles River Bridge. The grant allowed the ability to charge and collect tolls for 40 years (later extended to 70 years), after which the bridge was to be turned over to the state. Note that the Charles River Bridge Company had to compensate Harvard. There is a mixture of good sense, protectionism, and public finagling in the overall deal.

50. Patent Act of 1790, § 2.

5

Colonial Capitalism and the American Founding

CHRISTOPHER DEMUTH

The American founding was a momentous event in the development of modern government. It was similarly momentous in the development of modern capitalism. Our economic founding, however, was more evolutionary than revolutionary. By 1776, the 150-year colonial period had already generated a distinctive American capitalism. Political independence and the Constitution of 1787 gave that capitalism an institutional structure and a new purpose—to build a prosperous, democratic, continental nation.

The colonial era was a time of historic advances in manufacturing, finance, trade, and transportation, epitomized by the Dutch golden age of the 17th century and the first Industrial Revolution of the 18th century. The new ideas and practices originated in America's two progenitor nations, Great Britain and the Dutch Republic, and they accompanied the settlers to the New World. Here they were adapted and improved by a highly enterprising citizenry, surrounded by a staggering abundance of land and other natural resources, in circumstances that demanded creative improvisation and gave ample rein to commercial spirits.

By the later 1700s, Britain's American colonies had grown prosperous, with active markets, the widespread availability of credit, and, in the north, a substantial middle class. But the mother country remained bent on colonial mercantilism and political domination. Many of the grievances that precipitated the Revolution were economic and commercial, such as the British Trade and Navigation Acts running back to the 1620s, the settlement provisions of the Proclamation of 1763, the trade provisions of the Quebec Act of 1774, and various "taxes without representation." The short-lived Stamp Act of 1765 was a deeply resented imposition on commercial and property transactions in the colonies.

When independence had been won and the new nation began building its own political institutions, the founders faced many urgent questions of economic liberty, commercial regulation, and finance. The Constitutional Convention of 1787 was convened to address the Articles of Confederation's economic weaknesses—the national government's lack of authority over taxation, currency, foreign trade, and commercial quarrels within and among states. The Constitution included numerous provisions protecting property and contract, promoting domestic and foreign commerce, and ordaining limited government, which were enforced by early Supreme Courts. The first business of the Washington administration and the First Congress (other than drafting a bill of rights) was enacting import tariffs to promote domestic manufacturing and raise government revenue, funding continental and state war debts, and establishing a banking system and national currency.

In the 1982 predecessor to this volume—the American Enterprise Institute's (AEI) *How Capitalistic Is the Constitution?*[1]—the seven essayists agreed that the founding was capitalistic but disagreed over causes and consequences. Was our founding capitalism elitist and based on class (top-down) or democratic and populist (bottom-up)? How did this capitalism affect the course of American politics, society, and prosperity? How was it altered by subsequent events—wars and social movements, economic booms and busts, industrialization and urbanization, and the policy transformations of the Progressive and New Deal eras and the welfare state?

The AEI essayists used differing conceptions of "capitalism," a term that did not exist at the time of the founding. It came into the lexicon, and acquired a variety of systematic meanings, through the works of expositors from Karl Marx to Milton Friedman.[2] For instance, in the aftermath of the 2008–09 financial collapse, many progressive pundits announced that the event marked the "death of capitalism," necessitating financial socialism in its place; shortly thereafter, progressive economist Thomas Piketty argued that capitalism was not only alive but self-perpetuating, necessitating confiscatory wealth taxation.[3] In this chapter, I use the term to mean an economic system characterized by private property ownership, freedom of contract and association, market exchange, extensive division of labor in production, and well-developed banking and finance—with the key "capitalist" feature being profit-seeking financial markets that translate expectations about the future into current investments and consumption.[4]

In my view, the founders' government holds great lessons in capitalism for today's government.[5] It treated property and contract rights as a piece with political and personal liberties such as speech and religion—in contrast to the modern judicial practice of hiving off economic liberties and treating them as secondary.[6] It promoted private enterprise and commerce—rather than treating them as arenas of avarice in need of socializing.[7] It aimed to balance spending and revenues, reserve borrowing for investments and emergencies, and maintain a stable currency—economic disciplines now considered antediluvian.[8] I believe that these policies would be as beneficial today as they were 250 years ago and that intervening epochs have not antiquated them but rather demonstrated their enduring value.

These policies, however, were as controversial at the founding as they are today. "Crony capitalism," making sport of property and contract, was prevalent in the state legislatures both before and after the new Constitution.[9] Alexander Hamilton's debt and banking proposals were bitterly contested and enacted narrowly with a fair amount of political subterfuge.[10] Federalists and Jefferson Republicans differed vehemently on federal and state roles in economic policy.

Historian Ron Chernow notes that the founders

> inhabited two diametrically opposed worlds. There was the Olympian sphere of constitutional debate and dignified discourse—the way many prefer to remember these stately

figures—and the gutter world of personal sniping, furtive machinations, and tabloid-style press attacks. The contentious culture of these early years was both the apex and nadir of American political expression.[11]

But the rancorous politics was not just personal: It reflected deep differences among both founders and citizenry. The authors of the Declaration, Constitution, and state constitutions agreed on certain general principles concerning natural rights, private property, and market exchange but disagreed sharply on the application of those principles to practical questions.[12] The remarkable thing is that so many hotly debated issues were decided in ways that furthered a productive capitalist order and that, over time, the nation grew rich and powerful in the face of continuing disputes and uncertainties over economic policy, the enactment of many adverse policies, and shifting court interpretations of key constitutional provisions.

Just how did this happen? That is the fundamental question of the rise of cornucopian American capitalism. Quotations from the Declaration, the Constitution, the Federalist Papers, the founders' letters and diaries, and early court decisions can illuminate the question but cannot answer it.

Competitive Pluralism

The answer offered here is that America was founded in *competitive pluralism*. I use this coinage to distinguish it from the "liberal pluralism" that is sometimes said to be the essence of American nationhood—a mosaic of cultures, religions, and ethnicities peacefully coexisting in a spirit of mutual respect, or at least toleration, and cooperating for mutual advantage as circumstances warrant.[13] Competitive pluralism sees this diversity differently, as a dynamic—disparate institutions, traditions, and associations competing with one another for adherents, prestige, and prerogatives.

Liberal tolerance is an important feature of American pluralism, but the defining feature is energetic association building and proselytizing on behalf of matters moral and practical, personal and political. The national motto is not "Live and Let Live" but "E Pluribus Unum," with its dual meaning of individualism and collective striving for unity out of diversity.[14] Our pluralism has been competitive, rather than merely enterprising, because one man's enterprise has often come into conflict with the enterprises of others, and the resulting competition has been essential to revealing their respective value and generating improvement.

Competitive pluralism has been a critical source of vitality in American culture, science, and religion, enshrined in the First Amendment. It has also been the organizing principle of our politics, government, and commerce. In politics and government, multiple institutions compete for votes, jurisdiction, and power; in commerce, multiple suppliers compete for resources, workers, and customers.

The political and economic orders have a common provenance in our colonial heritage. Although the founders disagreed about many things, they were all suspicious of power and wary of its corruptions. Their hostility was born of experience with British[15] monarchs, aristocrats, and ministers and with their mercantilist trade restrictions and chartered business monopolies. For many of them, immediate experience was reinforced by the study of ancient history and contemporary philosophers from Montesquieu to Adam Smith. And once the War of Independence was won, there were no entrenched royals and aristocrats to push back.

That is not the whole story. The founders were also suspicious of political democracy and comfortable with hierarchy and meritocracy. But the British settlement of the Eastern Seaboard and western frontier had been localized, diverse, and entrepreneurial, led by pioneers who were accustomed to freedom of action and jealous of their prerogatives. When the time arrived for constructing a national Constitution, America was an adventitious regime of multiple, competing, self-made sources of authority. These sources had to be accommodated in some way. The entrenched interests pushed for decentralization rather than, as in Britain, centralization.

The founders were brilliant men, many of them highly learned and acutely conscious of their historic calling, and altogether singular in combining love of liberty with realism about human nature. Their Constitution deserves our reverential attention, assiduous study, and careful adherence. But America's founding economic order was not the product of abstract thinking and legal proclamation. Rather, it was a colonial inheritance of dispersed government, prosperous commerce, and personal assertiveness that shaped the founders' thinking and handiwork. Fragmented political power—competition in government—permitted men of commercial temperament and ambition, who were abundant in the colonies and new republic, to establish an economic order of competitive capitalism. American capitalism was the organic institutional embodiment of a society that had competition in its DNA.

Culture and Institutions

There is a rich debate over whether the primary determinants of economic prosperity are cultural or institutional. Proponents of the cultural explanation point to the norms and habits of individualism and personal agency, self-discipline and hard work, honesty and fair dealing, and forward thinking and positive-sum social cooperation.[16] Proponents of the institutional explanation point to laws and policies that facilitate investment and market transactions in a world (our world) of limited information and time, self-interested bias, and uncertainty about the future.[17] Both schools acknowledge that culture and institutions overlap and can reinforce each other for good or ill, and that proximate natural resources (fertile land, good harbors, energy, minerals) can be a boost.

A fair interpretation of this literature is that a favorable culture is necessary but not sufficient for economic prosperity: There are many examples of entrepreneurial cultures stymied by bad laws and policies (in China, for instance, and several nations in Latin America) but none of successful economies with favorable laws and adverse cultures. This is a useful construct for considering the emergence of American capitalism, which began with a highly auspicious cultural inheritance and found its way to exceptionally productive institutions.

Let us begin with Samuel Huntington (the scholar, not the founder):

> America's core culture has primarily been the culture of the seventeenth- and eighteenth-century settlers who founded our nation. The central elements of that culture are the Christian religion; Protestant values, including individualism, the work ethic, and moralism; the English language; British traditions of law, justice, and limits on government power; and a legacy of European art, literature, and philosophy. Out of this culture the early settlers formulated the American Creed, with its principles of liberty, equality, human rights, representative government, and private property.[18]

But the founding culture featured significant variations, and the principles of the American Creed were open to conflicting interpretations. David Hackett Fischer's *Albion's Seed* identifies four distinctive "folkways" that settlers brought from specific regions of the British Isles to specific regions of the American colonies.[19] Taking root in the world's first "voluntary society," they produced distinctive conceptions of freedom—the "ordered freedom" of the New England Puritans, the "reciprocal freedom" of the Pennsylvania Quakers, the "hegemonic freedom" of the Virginia cavaliers, and the "natural freedom" of the frontier backwoodsmen. Their differing beliefs and practices, including those regarding work, time, association, and wealth, led to social and sectional conflicts during the colonial period and then, with the nation building of the founding period, to the sharp political conflicts noted by Chernow and many others. Fischer shows that these political struggles—based on conflicting cultures rather than conflicting material interests—persisted throughout our history, up to the present day.

Hence competitive pluralism. The American settlers brought with them a core culture and set of political precepts that were sufficiently strong and uniform to form a nation worth fighting for. But they also brought many differences—and in the "voluntary society" and other unique circumstances of the New World, those differences confronted and competed with one another in a way they had not in the more hierarchical, less democratic Old World. The combination set the stage for a capitalist epoch in ways I now examine.

Colonial Culture and Circumstance

America was settled by adventurers, some of them well-off but fleeing religious persecution, some of them facing worldly problems and limited opportunities, some of them poor outcasts—all of them seeking a new life in a faraway land.[20] Well into the 18th century, the pilgrimage began with a perilous ocean voyage followed by daunting uncertainties and challenges. There was plenty of land and water, and eventually towns and a few cities, but making one's way would require hard work, resourcefulness, and resilience. They must have had an unusual appetite, or at least tolerance, for risk.

Moreover, life in the colonies required active commerce with Britain and Europe—trading furs, processed fish, farm produce, harvested timber, and other staples in exchange for manufactured goods (clothing, implements, and machinery), capital loans and investments, and "human capital" in the form of additional European settlers and African slaves. Alexis de Tocqueville's 1835 appraisal was that "nature and circumstances have made the inhabitant of the United States an audacious man; it is easy to judge of this when one sees the manner in which he pursues his fortune."[21] Historian Carl N. Degler's assessment in 1959 was that "capitalism came in the first ships."[22]

The enterprising spirit went beyond colonial merchants, artisans, and shopkeepers to include the large majority who were farmers and the numerous indentured servants (as were most British immigrants before 1700) who financed their migration and initial support with several years of contract labor.[23] Many of the early settler-farmers were preoccupied with sustaining themselves and their families and local communities, with little, if any, thought to producing a capitalist "surplus" for an impersonal market. But they were not hermits: They were perforce developers, and their local endeavors depended on trade, informal lines of credit among neighbors, and some degree of wealth accumulation over time. Those who put family, community, and moral obligation first sometimes saw colonial merchants, bankers, and politicians as akin to the labor-disdaining gentry of the Old World. Yet they, too, were making powerful contributions to an emerging American "democratic capitalism" by opposing vestiges of British class distinctions and making work rather than leisure the gauge of social status. That is the conclusion of an important pair of review essays by Gordon S. Wood in the 1990s.[24]

Religion in the New World. Many of the colonists were devoutly religious and imbued with the Protestant ethic of worldly duty and striving that Max Weber later identified as the spirit of capitalism.[25] While some colonies initially supported an established church, there was never a class of leisured clergy with lives and doctrines aloof from the quotidian concerns of their flocks. Instead, the dissenting denominations that arrived in America as religious refugees, and many new ones that sprang up here, were keenly attentive to the relations of the religious and the practical in their doctrines, and necessarily self-reliant and entrepreneurial in their secular lives.[26]

Among the earliest settlers, New England's Puritans were Calvinist, communitarian, and suspicious of some market practices—yet they had been allied in England with commercial interests in opposing royal prerogatives and came to America to establish a covenantal "city upon a hill" as agents of the Massachusetts Bay Company, a profit-seeking joint-stock company. John Winthrop was from a wealthy merchant family; in his many terms as Massachusetts governor, he supported Puritan "just price" doctrines but also a variety of economic development ventures, some of them with personal investments.

William Penn, also from a wealthy, well-connected family, was an equally fervent Quaker—he had been imprisoned several times for his convictions, once in solitary confinement in the Tower of London. He received an enormous colonial land grant from King Charles II, in part to pay off a debt to his father and in part to get him and his pestiferous religious followers far away from England. This apparently made Penn the world's largest private landowner. In this manner, Pennsylvania, like Massachusetts, was expected to be economically self-sustaining. The Quakers were more market friendly than the Puritans—Penn's position was that "though I desire to extend Religious freedom, yet I want some recompense for my trouble."[27]

Subsequent religious leaders, including Cotton Mather and Jonathan Edwards, were explicit that individual self-interest was not a mark of the Fall but rather intrinsic to God-given human nature: Properly restrained and disciplined, it encouraged man to love thy neighbor as thyself and to prosper God's creation.[28] Benjamin M. Friedman explains that this line of theology, in "accepting the moral legitimacy of self-interest while seeking a means of limiting and regulating it, was fully congruent with the view of competitive markets soon laid out by Adam Smith in *The Wealth of Nations*"—that is, the view that markets direct self-interest toward the interests of others.[29] Later American theologians connected the dots. In Wood's telling:

> Most of the evangelicals in these new religious associations [Baptists, Methodists, New Divinity Congregationalists, and dozens of other new sects] were not unworldly or anticapitalist. Quite the contrary: . . . [They] helped to make possible the rise of capitalism. Evangelical religious passion worked to increase people's energy as it restrained their selfishness, got them on with their work as it disciplined their acquisitive urges. . . . It gave people confidence that self-interested individuals nevertheless believed in absolute standards of right and wrong and thus could be trusted in market exchange and contract relationships.[30]

Equally important, the emergence of numerous denominational start-ups during the colonial period made institutional competition the defining characteristic of American religion. Some sects advocated religious tolerance, while others would have been happy with an Old World–style monopoly of their own. The conditions of colonial life settled the matter. The vast, sparsely settled territory made tidy parishes impossible. The population was culturally diverse and included many who were irreligious or mere deists. Economic development was imperative, so the opposition of many merchants and traders to religious preferences had to be accommodated. When enacted a century later, the First Amendment's protection of religious freedom was not a philosophical dispensation but rather a codification of facts on the ground.[31]

In these circumstances, even otherworldly, mammon-renouncing reformers were entrepreneurs in search of adherents who had many faiths competing for their souls. Historian Mark Häberlein notes that relations among the clergy of rival sects were often highly contentious. Although they came to "accept Protestant pluralism as congruent with their basic understanding of Christianity, toleration and cooperation did not diminish doctrinal differences. . . . The struggles over religious reform and authority in the competitive, religiously and ethnically diverse environment . . . led to a heightened sense of denominational identity."[32]

Tocqueville would emphasize a separate aspect of religious competition—that between church and state. Leaders of all faiths renounced involvement with government and secular politics, devoting themselves exclusively to promoting religious belief and observance, right behavior and good works. The result was that "in diminishing the apparent force of a religion one came to increase its real power." Privatized religion was a prime example of the American spirit of democratic equality and talent for voluntary organization, and "should therefore be considered as the first of their political institutions; for if it does not give them the taste for freedom, it singularly facilitates their use of it." Americans "so completely confuse Christianity and freedom in their minds that it is almost impossible to have them conceive of the one without the other"—they establish schools and universities and missionary churches on the frontiers so that the next generation may be "as free as the one from which it has issued."[33]

The Chief Business of the American Settlers. The British colonies were founded as either joint-stock companies owned by private investors (Massachusetts and Virginia) or royal land grants owned by individuals (the Carolinas, Georgia, Maryland, and Pennsylvania). New Netherlands was founded by the Dutch East India Company then seized by the British in 1664 and parceled out as royal land grants in what became New York, New Jersey, and parts of other colonies.[34] Most of the "charter colonies" and "proprietary colonies" were eventually converted to "royal colonies" formally governed by the Crown—but the land remained owned by the original grantees, and by the innumerable individuals and associations to whom they had conveyed parcels for purposes of settlement, under terms that were free of the royal obligations attached to landownership in Britain itself.[35] Colonial government generally consisted of a governor appointed by the king, a representative assembly of locally elected lawmakers, and loose supervision by the British Privy Council and Board of Trade in London.

Privatized, localized, for-profit colonization reflected English political traditions and, in the 17th century, the rise of the bourgeoisie[36] and the distracted circumstances of kings and ministers through decades of civil war and revolution. In contrast, the Spanish and French colonies were government projects, reflecting their (temporarily) greater wealth and stronger kings, an established Catholic Church, and the paltry political rights of their subjects. The Spanish came to America as conquistadores—conquerors and soldiers. The French came as trappers and merchants who, although organized as investor-owned companies for a time, were subjects of an absolute monarch with no political rights of their own. The difference was highly consequential.

Beyond immediate survival and subsistence, the British settlers were intent on economic improvement in a world rich in resources and potential but bereft of goods and credit, isolated by a mighty ocean, and bedeviled by weak local institutions, slow communications, and elemental risks. Many initial agriculture development projects failed miserably, as poorly informed London investors and overeager local agents learned expensive lessons in the geography, soil, and climate of the new territory and the ways of its native tribes. Territorial property rights were often hazy and contestable, leading to political intrigue in Westminster and Whitehall and inside dealing among fledgling colonial authorities. For security, commercial and financial ventures were often organized around trusted family members and coreligionists.[37] But that limited "the extent of the market" (Adam Smith)—the source of specialization and economic growth—that would await legal institutions to facilitate "transactions among strangers" (Douglass North).

Colonial Democratic Capitalism

Yet the colonies prospered. In the south, cultivation of tobacco for export and domestic sale was already succeeding in the 1620s, soon to be augmented by rice and other crops and then cotton.[38] During the same period, in New England and the south, lumbering trees from the immense forests for fuel, construction, and shipbuilding was equally successful.[39] Before long, sawmills had sprung up throughout the colonies, and by 1700, Boston was second only to London as a center of shipbuilding, outfitting booming fishing and shipping businesses.

Forestry was the original American "cowboy capitalism," combining rugged and adventurous living, skilled and dangerous work, and complex production and distribution. It also heralded colonial resistance to imperial mercantilism. The British Admiralty, impressed by the size and quality of New England white pine, forbade cutting them on public lands for anything but masts and spars for British ships. The edict was widely ignored and haphazardly enforced until the mid-1700s, when the government in London had finally gotten its North American act together following a century of domestic and European tumult. Britain then commenced serious enforcement of the edict—inciting violent reactions by New Hampshire backwoodsmen that, as Robert E. Pike recounts, "although not given much space in the history books . . . did more to cause the American Revolution than the Stamp Act and the tea tax put together."[40]

That is certainly an overstatement, but laissez-faire lumbering was part of an emerging colonial capitalism that was more democratic and free-wheeling than the inherited British form. The transformations came both by sea and by land.

By Sea. Transatlantic commerce was an urgent necessity that generated profound social and political changes, as Bernard Bailyn demonstrated in the first of his histories of early America.[41] The ambitions of Puritan leaders for a self-sufficient, theologically governed New England ran aground in the mid-1600s on failed efforts to establish domestic ironworks and manufacturers.[42] For the foreseeable future, the colony would be an extractive and agricultural economy, dependent on foreign trade. But ocean commerce required substantial capital investment and business acumen, reliable contacts in foreign ports, and financial arrangements for managing the enormous risks of sea transportation.

This led to the rise of the businessman on both sides of the Atlantic. In Britain, the first colonial expeditions were financed by wealthy gentry investors partnered with lowly moneygrubbing merchants—but when initial investments failed and had to be renegotiated, and new commercial arrangements became increasingly complex, the merchants came to dominate their less business-minded social betters.[43] In New England, merchants became respected, influential personages, equaling and eventually supplanting the Puritan gentlemen and church leaders in town government and, by the end of the 17th century, in colonial government.[44]

The merchants were a force for reforming the mercantilist policies and traditions of the mother country. From early colonial days, British navigation laws restricted foreign trade to British ships and ports—but the merchants impudently ignored them, trading actively with the French,

Dutch, and others. Their free trading continued until the years leading to the Revolution, when a British crackdown precipitated angry popular resistance akin to that caused by the timber restrictions. Colonial settlement grants, both joint stock and sole proprietor, contained numerous provisions giving trade monopolies to local authorities. These restrictions began as legitimate property rights to secure the investments of British underwriters, but they became unsustainable when the settlements developed from proprietorships into polities. Bailyn's account is worth quoting at length:

> In March 1635 . . . [the Massachusetts Puritan government] awarded to nine men representing nine towns around the Bay the exclusive right to board incoming ships, examine the goods, decide on the prices, and . . . buy the goods. . . .
>
> Such a restriction of access to incoming goods, however appealing it might have been to the Puritan magistrates, reflected more clearly the traditional English method of controlling trade by placing it exclusively in the hands of a responsible group whose rights and obligations were defined than it did the realities of life in New England. The exercise of such rights which might have formed the basis for a guild of merchants engaged in foreign trade required amounts of capital and an institutional complexity that did not exist in America. A law that demanded of other buyers that they stand by idly while nine fortunate individuals monopolized the middleman's profit could not be enforced. Moreover, the buying of goods sufficient to satisfy the needs of a whole town required ready money in amounts above that possessed by the nine assignees. And was it realistic to hope that supercargoes and sailors with goods to sell would limit sales to those men when others might pay more? Within four months of its enactment this law, which might have affected the society and economy of New England significantly, was repealed. . . .

> The group of importers which the Puritan magistrates failed
> to create by franchise grew independently. The key to its for-
> mation was credit, for it was by credit alone that the necessary
> goods were brought from Europe to America.[45]

This was a critical step from regimented monopoly capital to genera-
tive democratic capital—which would become, for 250 years, the quin-
tessence of American capitalism. It was helped along by the invention of
modern insurance.

Marine insurance, which had previously been ad hoc arrangements on
European and Middle Eastern trading routes, was first systematized in the
colonial transatlantic trade.[46] By the mid-1600s, this trade included not
only the approved England–North America routes but more complex itin-
eraries involving the West Indies, Macaronesia, and Spain, with exchanges
of cargo at every port. The multiple, compounding perils—tempests, navi-
gational complexities, sickness and other hazards to life and limb, lengthy
incommunicado time periods, and costly delays—focused the minds of
the merchants. They began to treat the risks as a commodity—separate
from the physical commodities being transported, subject to estima-
tion, valuation, and market exchange. During the 17th century, British
and American codes came to recognize "Merchants Assurances" against
"perils of the seas" and "acts of God." Some merchants specialized as
"merchant-underwriters," and exchanges were formed where insurance
contracts could be bought and sold.

Here was another commercial development with large cultural consequences. In historian Jonathan Levy's account, marine insurance led
to the American conception of freedom as self-ownership. If the future
could be reckoned with, rather than passively accepted as implacable fate,
then the individual should be responsible for his own life's course:

> In a democratic society, according to the new gospel, free and
> equal men must take, run, assume, bear, carry, and manage per-
> sonal risks. That involved actively attempting to become the

master of one's own personal destiny, adopting a moral duty to attend to the future.[47]

Levy examines the records of slave ships and court proceedings to show how this idea contributed to the abolition movement.[48] Slaves, like other seaborne commodities, had been insured by their owners. Could the shipowners recover their losses from an onboard slave revolt—or not, because the slaves had taken charge of their lives and attendant risks? If modern personhood meant self-mastery, then why shouldn't black persons be masters of their own selves?

America's emergence as a seafaring nation was driven by its competitive culture as well as business innovations. "United States ships," Tocqueville observed in the 1830s, "cross the seas most cheaply." He explained:

> The American is often shipwrecked; but there is no navigator who crosses the seas as rapidly as he does. Doing the same things as another in less time, he can do them at less expense.
>
> . . . The European navigator believes he ought to land several times on his way. He loses precious time in seeking a port for relaxation or in awaiting the occasion to leave it. . . .
>
> The American navigator leaves Boston to go to buy tea in China. He arrives in Canton, remains there a few days and comes back. In less than two years he has run over the entire circumference of the globe, and he has seen land only a single time. . . . He has drunk brackish water and lived on salted meat; he has struggled constantly against the sea, against illness, against boredom; but on his return he can sell the pound of tea for one penny less than the English merchant; the goal is attained.[49]

Tocqueville concluded that "Americans put a sort of heroism into their manner of doing commerce"—the American "not only follows a calculation, he obeys, above all, his nature."[50] This heartiness dated back at least to the founding period. In the 1770s, a British businessman in the Mediterranean Middle East groused, "Go where you will, there is hardly a petty harbor . . . but you will find a Yankee . . . driving a hard bargain with the natives."[51]

By Land. The colonists' most consequential economic innovation was converting the land from aristocratic endowment to democratic capital.

When Degler wrote that "capitalism came in the first ships," he meant, as mentioned earlier, that

> in early America . . . land was available to an extent that could appear only fabulous to land-starved Europeans. From the outset, as a result, the American who worked with his hands had an advantage over his European counterpart. For persistent as employers and rulers in America might be in holding to Old World conceptions of the proper subordination of labor, such ideas were always being undercut by the fact that labor was scarcer than land.[52]

He elaborates:

> Though land was not free for the taking, it was nearly so. In seventeenth-century New England there were very few landless people, and in the Chesapeake colonies it was not unusual for an indentured servant, upon the completion of his term, to receive a piece of land. Thus, thanks to the bounty of America, it was possible for an Englishman of the most constricted economic horizon to make successive leaps from servant to freeman, from freeman to freeholder, and, perhaps in a little more time, to wealthy speculator in lands farther west.[53]

The settlers made ready use of America's most abundant resource, in circumstances far removed from those that had shaped British property law.[54] The great land proprietors—recipients of royal grants and owners and managers of joint-stock companies—had a strong interest in remunerative settlement; so, too, did the emerging colonial governments, which gradually acquired authority over land distribution. They had to weigh immediate sales receipts against future returns from economic development. And they quickly learned that because land values were highly, often impossibly, speculative, development was the dominant consideration. That calculus aligned with the interests of the British government. Yale Law School professor Claire Priest explains:

> From the perspective of authorities in London, the colonies' role was to generate revenue for the Crown. Toward that end, British colonial land distribution policies encouraged immigration and settlement in North America by people who would actually inhabit the land and work the soil. Rather than granting land in vast parcels to a small group of elites, which was more typical in Spanish American colonies, in British America, the policy was to grant land directly to cultivators in small quantities.[55]

Colonial land was distributed by private arrangements or public sales and auctions, varying from place to place and time to time. But the dominant pattern was for parcels to be sold for low or nominal prices, often on easy credit, or given away outright in return for specific development commitments.[56] Liberal "headrights" granted heads of families ownership of 50 or 100 acres per family member and certain others—on condition that the grantees transport those persons to the land and build structures, improve the property, and meet other conditions by a certain date. These and larger grants were subdivided similarly—for example, a recipient would give away an acre in return for the construction of a sawmill. Or a township would be established by grant in return for building a community, and the township would in turn distribute small town parcels gratis to those who committed to living there.

Land was also occupied by outright squatting, which was illegal in Britain. The civil authorities and proprietary land titans, including Winthrop and Penn, regarded squatters as trespassers and banditti, a view that persisted into the 18th century (George Washington) and beyond (Henry Clay). But the practice was natural in an uncharted wilderness where "property rights" were a work in progress. The squatters, akin to those who held headrights and other concessionary grants, were populating the territory, cutting paths, building cabins and barns, clearing fields, planting crops, and endeavoring to become productive settlers. Settlers with ownership papers might themselves be quasi-squatters—their property specifications were often highly approximate, and they often claimed preferential rights to the use of adjacent land that was unclaimed or un-surveyed.

The squatters greeted eviction sheriffs with frontier defiance, but learned to manage their own property disputes by means short of force and violence. Over time, they fashioned rules and procedures for determining boundaries, tenures of possession, equity interests in cabins and crops, subdivision and transfer by sale or bequest, and other matters.[57]

Inexorably, their customs were adopted into official colonial law and legislation—some of them strikingly similar to headrights. Early on, a 1642 Virginia statute recognized what were later called "preemption rights": a squatter who had made improvements to a property could recover the value of the improvements from the rightful owner. If necessary, that value could be determined by a local jury and could result in the squatter receiving title to the property itself. Preemption rights were adopted in various forms by other colonies and were eventually joined by "settlement rights" that gave outright legal title to those who had settled unclaimed land.[58]

These innovations—wide and generous distribution of land as an inducement to settlement, governed by the settlers' own "natural law" recognized by courts and legislatures—democratized the colonies' greatest natural asset. They were radical departures from British practice, which had treated land as the foundation of hereditary social status and political stability, fenced off from the masses. Equally important were departures that transformed land into credit and currency in a society that badly needed both. That is the teaching of Priest's pathbreaking scholarship.

In her account, the departures were of two kinds, both accomplished in fits and starts over the colonial epoch amid constant controversy. The first was the creation of local (county) public records of land titles and mortgages, and courts of common pleas for resolving disputes over (among other things) landownership and creditor interests.[59] Public records and legal judgments borrowed from British institutions, but colonial authorities made them far simpler, cheaper, and more transparent. These elementary (to us) institutions formed the "backbone" of widespread property ownership, easy conveyancing, and routine use of land to facilitate private transactions. They were politically controversial because they were "the formal mechanism for protecting property rights, and essential foundation underlying the credit system and republican government"—established by representative assemblies and local councils asserting their independence from London authorities and royal governors.[60]

The second reform was expanding creditors' remedies against landowning borrowers. Public records of titles and mortgages, and simple judicial procedures for adjudicating property disputes, permitted creditors to establish repayment priorities against debtors who had fallen on hard times, disguised assets, or refused payments. More fundamentally, colonial legislation permitted creditors, in specified circumstances, to seize debtors' land in satisfaction of debts even if the land had not been pledged as security for the debts.[61] Previous histories had seen the American Revolution as inciting a revolution in land policy, aimed at rooting out remnants of British aristocratic tradition, accomplished through the founding-era wave of state abolition or reform of primogeniture and entail. (Primogeniture was the automatic conveyance of a decedent's family lands to the eldest male heir; entail was the protection of those lands against sale or seizure by creditors, to preserve them for undivided bequest to future generations.) Priest demonstrates that liberalizing creditor remedies— thereby transforming plenteous land into plenteous capital—began earlier, during the colonial period, and was powerfully motivated by economic considerations, not just republican political stirrings.

To explain: Colonies, at the outset, followed British law in distinguishing land from personal property and giving land unique protections. Much of the colonial land had been purchased on easy credit or promises of future performance, reflecting the dynamics described earlier. And, whether acquired by purchase, grant, or squatting, land was often borrowed against to finance development or consumption—farmers would purchase supplies and necessities from local merchants, for example, to be paid for by a portion of next fall's harvest. As a result, a considerable population was owed money or goods from neighbors, and complained when they discovered that their debtors' most valuable assets were legally unavailable to satisfy delinquent claims.

When the complaints reached the colonial assemblies, the politics was not a simple matter of creditors versus debtors, although it could come to that during economic downturns. The settlers were heavily dependent on credit for their livelihoods and currency. (IOUs could be passed around, as discussed in the next section.) They realized that businesslike legal remedies yielded more ample credit on better terms. Priest notes that measures to liberalize creditor remedies brought lower interest rates and that colonial officials understood that those measures expanded the availability of credit.

Moreover, many of the creditors were British. In 1732, following a recession in the Atlantic economy, Parliament enacted the Debt Recovery Act at the behest of British merchants with large colonial credit exposure.[62] The law made land, houses, and slaves available to satisfy creditors' claims in the American and West Indian colonies—but not in Britain itself. Colonial leaders were conflicted. They resented the British imposition of a uniform law on matters previously left to local legislation, but the act followed the legislative precedents of many colonies and kept the imported capital flowing.

Joseph Story, in his 1833 *Commentaries*, wrote that the colonial legal reforms made "land, in some degree, a substitute for money, by giving it all the facilities of transfer, and all the prompt applicability of personal property." He explained that "this was a natural result of the condition of the people in a new country, who possessed little monied capital; whose wants were numerous; and whose desire of credit was correspondently great"—and that "the growth of the respective colonies was in no small degree affected by this circumstance."[63] Priest goes further: The new legal structure

> made land more liquid, more extendable as collateral, and more readily available as a source of investment capital. This legal shift fundamentally transformed the economic, political, and social structure of the colonies. . . .
>
> The most important effect was to diminish the role of landed inheritance in American society by privileging the claims of creditors over heirs when debtors died.[64]

The emergence of an American "credit nation" was a complicated story with a dark side. During economic downturns, colonial assemblies could abruptly replace credit-promotion policies with debtor-protection policies that left creditors in the lurch (which was what prompted London's Debt Recovery Act). Not only land but enslaved persons were commodified and pledged as collateral for plantation loans; the expansion of creditor remedies contributed to the vigorous 18th-century growth of the slave economy and the particular horror of slave auctions to satisfy debts.[65]

But converting the land to democratic capital shaped the colonial political economy in two critical respects. First, it introduced commercial considerations into the everyday lives of large numbers of settlers. Not only merchants and shopkeepers but farmers, artisans, and townsfolk learned to balance accounts, and to balance consumption and investment, as practical means of managing the risks of an unsettled world. A people who had been self-selected for their tolerance for risk were devising institutions that harnessed that tolerance for economic, social, and political improvement.

Second, it exemplified the American practice of bottom-up nation building by local initiative and institutional competition. Colonies with disparate cultures and natural endowments adjusted their laws to attract settlers and promote growth. In so doing, they were building a nation of strong regional sovereignties that would soon become states.

Both developments were fortified by a complementary innovation, that of paper money.

Mediums of Exchange

There was an important weakness in colonial capitalism: a shortage of currency and, until the 1700s, an almost total absence of banks. This was, in part, an aspect of the times—even in Britain and Holland, money and banking were far less developed in 1700 than they would be a century hence. But it was primarily a matter of British policy, which suppressed finance in its colonies and led the colonists to improvise in ways that were characteristically enterprising and localized, setting the stage for the American capitalism to come.

For much of the colonial period, British authorities restricted the export of specie (silver and gold money) from the homeland. They also restricted the colonies from coining their own money and establishing banks; at the same time, British merchants usually required payment in specie from colonial purchasers. These practices were central prongs of mercantilism, which held that the purpose of colonial expansion was to stockpile treasure in the mother country. Indeed, mercantilism began as bullionism, aiming narrowly to find, mine, and import foreign silver and gold for purposes of financing wars and other royal initiatives. With the growth of global trade in the 1500s and early 1600s, the doctrine evolved into a more modern form: The purpose of colonization was to produce a positive balance of trade for headquarters. Jonathan Barth's vivid history of British mercantilism notes:

> By the early part of the seventeenth century, the balance-of-trade doctrine enjoyed near-universal acceptance among

economic theorists, retaining its prized position as the central pillar of economic thought for the next 150 years. . . . Mercantilist policymakers demanded coin even more than their bullionist predecessors. [They] simply better understood now how best to acquire it and then how to retain it. . . . "Trade is a richer and more dureable Mine than any in Mexico or Peru," declared [one] writer in 1696.[66]

For the first century of colonization, when British authorities were frequently engulfed in problems at home, they enforced money and banking restrictions as haphazardly as trade restrictions such as the Navigation Acts. Massachusetts began minting its own silver currency in 1652 without seeking permission—the "pine-tree shilling," provocatively bearing a symbol of both the colonial frontier and an economic product of special value to the British Admiralty. Westminster complained and threatened but let the practice continue for 30 years, closing the mint in 1682 when its proprietor retired.[67] But when Maryland in 1659 and New York in 1675 asked for permission to establish mints, the answer was no.[68]

The colonists were able to get their hands on some foreign specie, especially Spanish dollars ("pieces of eight") from trade with the West Indies, but these were often transshipped to Britain as payment for imports. With insufficient hard currency for a growing domestic economy, they resorted to private money substitutes that were better than barter (swapping x hens for y yards of cloth) but vastly inferior to the real thing.[69] "Commodity money"—tobacco in the south and corn and other staple goods ("country pay") in the north—was widely used but physically cumbersome, hard to standardize, and subject to swings in value from good and bad harvests and shifts in consumer demand.

Closer to modern currency was the use of debt—IOUs—as money. Merchants and individuals known to each other exchanged goods and services for credit and kept careful book accounts (a practice facilitated by adding land to creditors' remedies). "Bills of obligation" and "promissory notes"—documents backed by commodity reserves or other resources, promising repayment in goods or services at a given date—circulated as money. But as Priest explains, their "circulation was likely to extend only as far as the reputation of the payor"; like books of account, they "functioned within the context of relatively small communities."[70] Another shortcoming was that notes and book accounts did not establish a uniform unit of exchange—a key benefit of denominated money—because the amounts due were based on individually negotiated transactions. So the early colonists lacked a price metric for comparing costs and opportunities across markets, regions, and time.

By the late 1600s, these expedients were no longer keeping pace with growing economies and growing demands on government, especially military demands. Thereupon the colonial governments began to "emit" official paper money (the conventional term in these matters), both directly and through rudimentary banks.[71] Much of it was "fiat money," meaning it could not be exchanged on demand for specie or other tangible assets: The paper had no intrinsic value other than government imprimatur and, sometimes, a "legal tender" requirement that it be accepted as payment for debts and purchases. It was the first modern paper currency, another profound capitalist invention of the American colonials.[72] It emerged over several decades, step by step, from individual responses to local events.

The first of these steps illustrates the element of serendipitous discovery. In 1690, a Massachusetts military expedition intending to seize Quebec from France failed disastrously, leaving the government with heavy debts and mutinous returning soldiers who had expected to be paid in victor's plunder. In desperation, the assembly offered the soldiers "bills of credit," promising to redeem the bills in specie or tangible tax revenues when available (there were none at the time), in the meantime promising to accept the bills for tax payments. The promises were doubtful at a tumultuous time—Massachusetts had lost more than 1,000 soldiers in the Quebec debacle, the British had recently closed the pine-tree shilling mint and were in the process of revoking the colony's royal charter, and the Salem witch trials were about to commence (in 1692). Many of the soldiers, equally desperate, took the bills of credit and sold them at a heavy discount for "country pay" or other goods.

And then the bills began to circulate as money. They had not been designated "money" or "legal tender"—which might have aroused opposition from London at a delicate time—but they were cleverly issued in small denominations on pocketable notepaper. Although the appearance of paper money was controversial, many colonial leaders were advocating government currency to facilitate trade, and some merchants offered to back the bills' redemption value with specie of their own. The bills soon recovered their economic value and proved to be highly popular. After a new charter had been obtained from London in 1692, Massachusetts issued additional bills of credit annually, made them legal tender for private transactions as well as tax payments, and promised to redeem them from new tax revenues at specified future dates.

Most of the other colonies followed Massachusetts's lead in the early and mid-1700s. Often they, too, were financing military emergencies. (Virginia, a paper-money holdout, finally resorted to bills of credit in 1755 during the French and Indian War.) But some colonies emitted currency to pay routine government debts and purchases and to launch development projects. Others, predominantly Pennsylvania during a local economic depression in 1723, did so purely to promote economic growth and attract new settlers; these emissions, unconnected to government expenditures, were sometimes offered to those who could secure them with land and property and sometimes distributed per capita to all taxpaying citizens.

In addition, the colonies established "land banks" or "land offices," which were essentially mortgage companies that made loans secured by real estate. The loans typically were for half the value of the pledged property, charged below-market interest rates, and were spent in the first instance on property improvements and other investments. These were secured loans from governments to citizens—in contrast to bills of credit issued as payment for military and other services, which were unsecured loans from citizens to governments. Both employed debt as a basis of currency; they were like the private money of books of account and bills of obligation but with advantages of scale, ease of use among far-flung strangers, and official units of account. Several private associations also issued bills of credit secured by land mortgages—America's first private banks.[73]

The terms of the paper moneys varied widely among colonies and over time. They carried shorter and longer redemption periods; some were legal tender, and some were not; some paid interest, while others did not. Maryland's currency was paper but not "fiat"—it was redeemable in specie on deposit in London. The economic results also varied widely. In Massachusetts, overissuance produced severe price inflation between 1720 and 1750, reducing the colony at times to a near barter economy.[74] Other colonies, including the Carolinas, mismanaged their currencies to lesser degrees; New Jersey and New York performed relatively well; and Pennsylvania was a paragon of stable money.

The worst of these episodes have been offered as examples of the political seduction of ever-depreciating fiat money, favoring debtors at the expense of creditors.[75] But "monetary policy" (a term that did not, of course, exist at the time) was new, uncharted territory and involved a good deal of novice trial and error. Shortage of currency was a nearly universal complaint.[76] Merchants and other creditors were leading proponents of generous money emissions to lubricate trade and limit consumer debt.[77] Most of the colonial economies were growing much of the time, but no one had any idea of actual or potential growth rates or how much new money would accommodate, stimulate, or suppress growth. The complex, poorly understood interrelationships of currency terms, quantity, value, velocity, and foreign trade made for many surprises. When governments postponed promised redemption dates, either to keep bills in circulation or defer raising taxes to fund their redemption, the bills' value would fall because of the reneging; when governments stuck with redemption dates, bills would disappear from circulation, hoarded for an upcoming payday.

What the colonists did have was a gradually accumulating knowledge about money from their experiences with numerous competing approaches, and the results improved over time until the desperate monetary emissions to finance the Revolutionary War. In the meantime, the new bills circulated widely, often into neighboring colonies, displacing specie and money substitutes and establishing the modern world's first paper cash economies. Because of their varying terms and stability, they did not provide a uniform unit of exchange across colonies nor a store of value for those who held them. But they were a serviceable, growth-expanding means of exchange within and between the colonies.

For all its shortcomings, paper money was a brilliant adaptation to colonial circumstances.[78] In an underdeveloped economy with little wealth but strong potential, financing public exigencies with debt rather than taxes—to be repaid when the tax levies were a smaller burden on a larger economy—was a sensible course. Government borrowing for military and economic emergencies and for investment in durable infrastructure are canonical practices of sound public finance.[79] Borrowing for routine expenditures is a no-no in a developed economy, but that was not true in the colonial economies-in-progress where immediate necessities often exceeded available resources.

For private markets, paper currency was an astute solution to the lack of mobile, tangible capital. With limited supplies of the traditional monetary asset of silver and gold coin, the colonists turned to two alternative assets that were in ample supply. The first was the tangible but immobile asset of land, whose abundance was observable to everyone, stretching endlessly to the west. Land became easily divisible, transferable, and usable as security through the legal reforms described in the previous section; it was converted to neighborhood currency through private books of account and bills of obligation and then to mobile currency through the monetary emissions of the land offices.

The second was the intangible, mobile asset of debt—which constitutes confidence in the future. That confidence was the only asset behind a merchant's sale of goods for a portion of next year's harvest or on the customer's trustworthy reputation; behind a government's bills of credit to soldiers or other suppliers, promising to pay them from future resources; and behind a government's distribution of bills in the expectation that recipients would use them productively. Basing currency on optimism is risky. It has often come to grief, including in the periods of high colonial price inflation, and it was promiscuously abused in subsequent stages of American capitalism. But the colonists were right to trust in the American promise of freedom and improvement that had brought most of them here in the first place. As discussed in coming sections, that trust was vindicated by the Revolution and then formalized by Hamilton's program of national debt assumption, money, and banking in the new republic.[80]

Paper money was also an adaptation to the British restrictions. The British could hardly object to bills of credit to finance participation in their colonial wars, and indeed those emissions were sometimes retroactively funded by British specie payments. More generally, paper money was a new phenomenon in the annals of colonial mercantilism. It reduced the demand for specie for domestic transactions, leaving more available for purchasing British imports. (The counterparties were specializing in their preferred forms of money—specie for one, land and debt for the other.) But money issued by "banks" was suspect, because banking was considered a prerogative of the mother country. (Some colonies called their mortgage banks "land offices" to avoid censure.) Beyond the doctrinal uncertainties, the British were as inexpert as the colonists in the forms and consequences of monetary emissions, which led to much confusion, vacillation, and mutual ill will.[81]

The one consistency in British policy was acute responsiveness to the complaints of London's merchant-creditors when colonial paper was depreciating sharply, as in Massachusetts in the 1730s and 1740s. In that case, the British authorities issued strenuous orders for massive redemptions of bills of credit with new taxes, which the colonists knew would be disastrous. Then Britain shuttered the colony's land bank, which had been a force for monetary stability because its bills were tied to land values. And then came another serendipity. Following a joint military attack on a French fort in 1744 (this one successful), the British withdrew their tax-and-redeem order and paid Massachusetts a large sum in specie for its costs of the operation—whereupon the colonists, of their own accord, used the payment to put their currency on a hard specie standard. That reversed the radical depreciation of the past 30 years in a stroke, and Massachusetts joined Pennsylvania as a stable-money economy.

Official paper currency was, however, a political as well as economic innovation, substantially increasing the size and scope of government.[82] Purchasing with bills of credit, whether for investments, emergencies, or routine operations, is deferred taxation. The government acquires additional responsibilities today to be paid for tomorrow, after the new responsibilities are faits accomplis, from future taxes on (if all goes well) wealthier and more numerous taxpayers. The procedure thereby paves the way for bigger government and higher taxes than most citizens would assent to at the outset. (The colonists were highly averse to both.) Moreover, it spreads the public debt widely in small lots; the alternative, selling long-term bonds in large denominations, creates a class of creditors to monitor government on behalf of fiscal rectitude, with greater motivation and organization than average voters.[83] (The colonists were highly suspicious of organized finance, viewing it as a source of corruption rather than discipline.) Most of all, controlling of the medium of exchange injects government into citizens' daily lives and fortunes, exercised by calibrating taxing, spending, borrowing, and redemption with newfound political discretion.

Many colonial merchants and thought leaders favored government money to relieve consumers of taking on too much personal debt as a means of exchange. What it did, however, was concentrate debt in the government at higher per capita levels than individuals could prudently assume. That was beneficial in establishing a regime of widely circulating money, but only to the extent the government managed the debt responsibly. And that task combined intrinsic complexity with new forms of politics. The colonial governments became immersed in managing conflicting financial interests among differently situated citizens, among different colonies (the money policies of one colony could interfere with those of neighboring colonies), and between the colonies and Great Britain. The conflicts with Britain were key progenitors of the Revolutionary War.[84]

Those within and among colonies fostered the growth of active, decentralized structure of government that awaited the framers of the Articles of Confederation and the Constitution.

Comes the Revolution

On the eve of the War of Independence, Britain's North American colonies, 150 years from an unsettled wilderness, had grown exceptionally prosperous. Our measures are approximate—economic surveys were nonexistent, and the first census came in 1790 under the new Constitution. But historians and economists who have studied records of wages, land sales, business and household purchases, imports and exports, and slave and indentured-servant contracts have found that the settlers' material circumstances were among the best in the world. Their incomes and living standards were much higher than in Britain and Europe (excepting the top of old-world royalty and aristocracy), and even higher than in Latin America and French Canada (with the short-lived exception of Barbados and perhaps other sugar islands).[85] Income distribution was unusually equal, and more than 70 percent of New England families owned their own land. Energy (wood and watercourses) was abundant, health status was good for the era, diets were rich and nutritious, and food was efficiently distributed in the port cities.[86]

Reflecting these conditions, the average stature of men was 5'9", about three inches taller than their British and European counterparts.[87] And the population was booming—it grew from roughly 50,000 in 1640 to one million in the 1740s and then doubled to more than two million by the 1770s. This was due in part to net immigration but mostly to native increase through extraordinarily (for the era) high birth rates and long lifespans.[88]

The colonial economy was also becoming more diversified and self-sufficient. The domestic manufacturing that had baffled the early settlers was succeeding and replacing imported goods. By the 1750s, at least 80 iron furnaces in the colonies were producing about as much iron as

Britain was, and some of it was even exported to the mother country. Foreign trade—now carried primarily in American ships—remained bustling, but its composition was changing: Benjamin Franklin and other leaders worried that the colonists were now importing foreign "luxuries" rather than "necessities" and that consumerism threatened republican virtue and family savings. In other words, the colonists were producing more of their own necessities, and their standards of living were rising.[89]

Yet republican virtue appears to have been thriving as well. In New England, an informal network of civic, religious, family, and commercial institutions was decisive in resisting Britain's initial military forays in 1775, culminating in the Battles of Lexington and Concord—orchestrated by Paul Revere, artisan of silver luxuries.[90]

The colonists had made the most of their British (and Dutch) political, legal, religious, cultural, and commercial traditions. A long period of lax British oversight had permitted them to adapt those traditions to a world of endless territory, natural riches, and social space for personal initiative and to establish representative assemblies and town councils unknown to their forebears. The other American colonies—British and Dutch as well as Spanish and French—featured one or a few of these circumstances, but none featured all of them. It was in British North America that they all came together, with astonishing results.

That assessment is fortified by empirical research into the "origin factors" of colonial prosperity at the time of the American founding and down to the present day. These studies evaluate the economic consequences of

- Case-by-case British common law, as opposed to prescriptive French civil law;[91]

- Economic integration with British markets, where wages were much higher than in Spain;[92]

- A healthy climate, which attracted large numbers of permanent settlers from Britain and Europe;[93]

- Local conditions favoring social equality and widespread landownership, which produced a politics of equal opportunity and public investment;[94] and

- The simple fact of colonization by Britain rather than other powers.[95]

The factors overlap, and the authors have their disagreements over causal importance, similar to those in the broader literature on "culture" versus "institutions" discussed earlier.[96] For our purposes, what is clear is that all the factors coincided in one and only one place: the colonies that were to become the United States. Notably, the only comparably prosperous colonists were Canadians—but only British Canadians, with French Canadians lagging far behind.[97]

The Revolutionary War came at a terrible cost, documented in Deirdre Nansen McCloskey's contribution to this volume.[98] More American lives were lost per capita than in any subsequent war, incomes fell drastically, and the continental and many state governments were bankrupted. The rebelling colonies lost the tremendous economic benefits of participation in the British Empire, including favorable within-empire trade arrangements and London-financed defense against seaborne pirates, indigenous tribes, and rival French and Spanish colonizers. Those benefits certainly outweighed the costs of lethargic colonial mercantilism in the 1600s. In the 1700s, a renascent Great Britain began seriously enforcing trade, financial, and political restrictions and became embroiled in several costly wars in important North American theaters. But even then, as McCloskey and other historians have noted, the costs to the colonies of the Stamp Act and other British impositions were a pittance compared with the costs of the resulting war and the taxes the new nation would soon impose on itself.

What seems to have happened is this: First, in the 1600s settlement period, the combination of English protections, liberal land grants, and loose colonial supervision produced a national incubator where the colonists grew their own political and economic institutions, with interests and values increasingly separate from those of the mother country. Then, in the 1700s prewar period, those differences became profound and irreconcilable. Britain had become an assertive, debt-ridden, extravagantly extended colonial power, while the colonists had built prosperous societies with governments capable of mobilizing their distinctive interests and values. The commercial and financial disputes that led to revolution were not about the economic costs of the British policies—they were about the colonists' desire to govern themselves. Here is Captain Levi Preston, a veteran of the Battles of Lexington and Concord, in an 1843 interview:

> "Were you oppressed by the Stamp Act?"
>
> "I never saw any stamps and I always understood that none were ever sold."
>
> "Well, what about the tea tax?"
>
> "Tea tax, I never drank a drop of the stuff, the boys threw it all overboard."
>
> "But I suppose you have been reading Harrington, Sidney, and Locke about the eternal principle of liberty?"
>
> "I never heard of these men. The only books we had were the Bible, the Catechism, Watts' psalms and hymns and the almanacs."
>
> "Well then, what was the matter?"
>
> "Young man, what we meant in going for the Redcoats was this: we always had governed ourselves and we always meant to. They didn't mean we should."[99]

While the colonists appeared to the British to be spoiled brats (at least the rebels among them), what they really were was freedom-loving settlers with a 150-year history of successful (on the whole) entrepreneurial risk-taking. If they had been poorer, or had had weaker governments, or if more of them had been conventionally risk averse like the Tories among them and the British Canadians to the north, they would have stuck with the colonial bargain. But they had become a polity, a proto-nation, that was willing to take the enormous gamble of charting an independent course. And they had the resources to make a fight of it.

The war itself was an economic catastrophe but also a spur to many lasting improvements in production. Faced with the loss of British imports, a British naval blockade, and the urgency of arming and provisioning an army, the Americans established new industries and improved manufacturing methods in textiles, iron, arms and ammunition, shipbuilding, tools, and agriculture and began to integrate regional markets. They forged new financial arrangements with the Dutch and French. Their entrepreneurial exploits complemented their military exploits in defeating the British.[100]

The war was also the testing ground for dissimilar colonial cultures to work together for national goals. Upon taking command of the Continental Army in Cambridge, Massachusetts, in 1775, General Washington, Virginia cavalier par excellence, had an *Albion's Seed* moment, observing in dismay the radically different ways of New England individualists, Pennsylvania democrats, and backwoods roughnecks. Following his army's terrible defeats at the battles around New York City in July–November 1776, he fashioned a style of leadership that bore its first fruits in the victories of Trenton and Princeton in December and January.

It was in sharp contrast to the dictatorial British generalship he had observed as a colonial officer in the French and Indian War, where the commanding officer would convene a council of war to announce his battle plans and parcel out assignments to silent, often privately dissenting subordinates. Washington would instead open his councils with a review of circumstances, opportunities, and constraints, then preside open-mindedly over a vigorous debate among generals and colonels, and occasional guest civilians, of the pros and cons of different strategies, at length concluding with his own assessment and battle plan.[101] This was the beginning of his "team of rivals" approach to political leadership that, as president, he deployed among Thomas Jefferson, Hamilton, and other officials, and that presidents Abraham Lincoln, Franklin D. Roosevelt, and Ronald Reagan would later adopt.[102] It may fairly be described as democratic, in contrast to the hierarchical, class-infused style of

British generalship, but its essential strength was open competition as a means of discovering and interpreting available information about an uncertain situation.[103]

The Colonial Inheritance at the Founding

Immediately upon the adoption of the Constitution in 1787 and the establishment of its new government in 1788–90, the US economy began to grow dramatically faster than it had during the colonial period. From 1660 to 1780, a hypothesized colonial gross domestic product (GDP), estimated with the procedures mentioned earlier, grew by about 3–4 percent annually, about 0.2–0.5 percent per capita.[104] Then, in the 1790s, year-to-year GDP growth surged to 6 percent, 3 percent per capita; from 1800 to 1860, until the Civil War, GDP growth continued at an average annual rate of 4 percent, 1 percent per capita.[105]

Economic growth after the adoption of the Constitution was also considerably higher than in Britain and Europe and in their remaining American colonies.[106] It was powered by newfangled business corporations that had barely existed before: banking and insurance; firms building roads, bridges, and canals; and manufacturing.[107] Domestic markets became increasingly specialized and integrated across regions, and exports boomed.[108] The population grew even faster than in the late colonial period—from 3.9 million in 1790 to 5.3 million in 1800, then to 12.9 million in 1830 and 31.4 million in 1860. Much of the population went west and settled three new states by 1800, another seven by 1820, then 10 more by 1860.

The burst of economic energy was no doubt precipitated by the Constitution itself and the new government's policies. The Constitution established strong protections for property and contract, specified a system of property rights in inventions in "science and the useful arts," and enabled the federal government to negotiate the first nationwide trade and navigation agreements with foreign nations. The Washington administration and the First Congress established a largely private national banking system and a reputable national currency with uniform units of account. The Constitution gave business-minded citizens the confidence "to invest significant sums of their own money in risky, large-scale enterprises."[109] The immediate deployment of a banking system, national currency, and securities markets appears to have been essential to rapid commercial expansion and national development.[110]

Moreover, the Constitution's authors were strongly committed to private enterprise in practice and crafted a document that gave it a wide berth. In *How Capitalistic Is the Constitution?*, Mark F. Plattner shows that the founders, represented by the three who penned the Federalist Papers, favored "an economic system that allows all citizens freely to acquire, possess, and dispose of private property and encourages them to devote themselves to the pursuit and enjoyment of wealth." To them, "increasing national wealth" was desirable for political and economic reasons: "Encouraging individuals to pursue their own private gain becomes a means toward promoting the public good," while "the avarice stimulated by commerce, though undeniably a selfish passion, is nonetheless conducive to habits of industry, prudence, and sobriety—in short, to the regularity of morals."[111]

Genesis and Prelude. The founders' words, deeds, and purposes were not thunderbolts from heaven or philosophical treatises. They had a specific, practical genesis—their colonial inheritance of do-it-yourself enterprise and institutional competition. That inheritance was personified in the founders themselves. Most of the signers of the Declaration and Constitution were accomplished men of commerce—merchants and farmers, shippers and shopkeepers, investors and speculators, and land developers—albeit wealthier and more educated and learned than most.[112] These included Washington, Franklin, John Hancock, Robert Morris, James Wilson, and many lesser figures.[113] Political philosopher James Madison, lawyer John Adams, and aristocrat Jefferson were not businessmen, but all three, like Franklin, were avid, empirically minded students of science.[114] Hamilton was an immigrant and self-made lawyer and military officer, had litigated landmark commercial cases during the Articles of Confederation period, and was a brilliant student of finance. Most of the founders, who like Hamilton and Adams, were primarily lawyers, politicians, and pamphleteers, had substantial commercial backgrounds: John Dickinson, great-grandson of a Virginia indentured servant, was one of the largest landowners and richest citizens of the new nation; John Jay was from a prominent merchant family; and Gouverneur Morris was from a family of wealthy landowners.

These men were utterly unlike the leaders of most revolutions—radical intellectuals, malcontent lawyers, romantic noblemen, and ambitious military officers. Such were the members of the Committee on Public Safety in the contemporaneous French Revolution, none of whom had any significant experience in commerce and trade.[115] In contrast, the American revolutionaries, accustomed to the give-and-take of business affairs, were pragmatic, comfortable with competing interests, and amenable to compromise. America was blessed to have been founded by leaders of a society that had yet to generate elites aloof from the concerns of everyday life and contemptuous of social tradition. They were products of a world they had built for themselves, a world they wished to preserve and improve rather than overthrow.[116]

Their colonial inheritance came of age under the Articles of Confederation (1781–89). That is not the usual characterization of the 1780s, which are generally regarded as a lost decade of political and economic chaos that came close to forfeiting the promise of national independence. Chaos there surely was. The economy was in a serious depression—largely the aftermath of a ruinous war, including the devastation of urban trading centers and river towns and the expatriation of many Tory merchants.[117] Two major defects of the Articles of Confederation contributed to the chaos—the Confederation Congress's lack of authority to tax, which left it without resources to pay soldiers and other suppliers or to stem the hyperinflation of the war years, and its inability to negotiate commercial treaties, which led to a sharp decline in foreign trade.

Yet even in the face of these troubles, the colonial spirit of enterprise was showing its stuff and making good use of its new independence. In a work of economic reconstruction famous among specialists, Winifred Barr Rothenberg showed that in the 1780s, New England farm prices first began to converge across the region and move in tandem through temporal ups and downs. Her discovery was the economic equivalent of the monolith in Arthur C. Clarke's 2001: A *Space Odyssey*—pointing to the formation of extended markets. Farm output began to grow, both per worker and per acre (and without the impetus of new technology), and farmers began to shift marginal resources from livestock and implements to financial assets.[118] Wood elaborates:

> It is not surprising . . . that Rothenberg should have located the emergence of a rural New England market economy in the 1780s. For the 1780s were . . . the most critical moment in the entire history of America. The few years following the end of the War of Independence clearly revealed for the first time all the latent commercial and enterprising power of America's emerging democratic society. In the 1780s we can actually sense the shift from a premodern traditional society to a modern one in which the business interests and consumer tastes of ordinary people were coming to dominate. Something momentous was happening in the society and culture that released the aspirations and energies of common people as never before in American history, or perhaps in world history. The American Revolution with its declaration that all men were created equal and had the inalienable rights to life, liberty, and the pursuit of happiness became an expression and justification of this release of aspirations and energies.[119]

Corroborating evidence: The American population surged by 41 percent in the 1780s—a higher rate of growth than any decade after the 1660s and any decade since—and "the number of nonbusiness corporations such as municipal governments, churches, and voluntary associations expanded rapidly."[120]

The reputation of state and national government under the Articles of Confederation has suffered from the animadversions of the promoters of the 1787 Philadelphia Convention and its Constitution. Prominent among them were several of Madison's and Hamilton's *Federalist* essays[121] and Madison's April 1787 tract "Vices of the Political System of the United States."[122] The criticisms of the Confederation government's lack of tax, monetary, and treaty powers (especially over trade agreements) were well-taken, widely recognized, and promptly addressed by and under the Constitution. But other criticisms were unsupported, overstated, or oblivious to the beneficial forces at work in a decentralized, state-centered political system.

The Confederation Congress, for all its weaknesses, turned in an outstanding legislative and diplomatic record. Because it voted by state and required a supermajority of nine states, its actions exemplified competitive collaboration for national goals. The Articles of Confederation required full unanimity for ratification, which obliged the states with extensive claims to western territory (primarily Virginia, the Carolinas, and Georgia) to relinquish their claims to the national government, implicitly for the formation of additional, smaller states. The states without western claims were anxious; Maryland stood firm, and after several rounds of hard bargaining the claimant states agreed to cede their land sufficiently to bring Maryland along.[123] The Congress proceeded to conclude peace negotiations and ratify the Treaty of Paris in 1784, in which Britain ceded nearly all of its non-Canadian land, nearly doubling US territory.

So the fledgling government began revenue poor but land rich. The universal expectation was that it would sell land to pay off Revolutionary War debts. But the idea ran into the same problem that had confronted the initial colonial landowners in the 1600s: The value of the unsettled land was highly speculative, and the profit-maximizing strategy was to pursue economic and political development rather than immediate sale. That required patience and vision, and the Congress came through.

Its Land Ordinances of 1784 and 1785 and Northwest Ordinance of 1787 were stunning legislative achievements. Together, they established a highly successful system for surveying and parceling the territorial land in grids, creating townships with property reserved for schools, and selling or granting manageable plots in perpetual fee simple, building on the legal reforms of the colonial period. Once again, the abundant land was shrewdly capitalized. The ordinances also made rules and procedures for chartering new states with sizes and populations consistent with those of the founding 13; laid down protections of property, political, and religious freedoms anticipating those of the Constitution and Bill of Rights; and forbade slavery in the Northwest Territory. Along the way, the Confederation Congress established a startup network of post offices and post roads and was represented in foreign capitals by the likes of Adams, Franklin, Jay, and Jefferson.

The founders who regarded the national legislature as pitifully impotent regarded the state legislatures as perniciously potent—dominated by small-minded, "middling" persons (many of them unlearned businessmen) unrestrained by either personal morality or government structure from proliferating laws for selfish "factional" advantage.[124] Those legislatures were indeed scenes of the majoritarian passions the founders feared, but the major cases in point were instances of angry postwar recrimination and turmoil—bills of attainder convicting named Tory loyalists of treason and confiscating their property, and ex post facto laws permitting debtors to pay creditors (including Washington) with badly depreciated currency. These practices would be forbidden by the Constitution without substantive objection.[125] The states' minoritarian, "special interest" practices included granting monopoly privileges to chartered corporations—which continued under the Constitution, eventually to be reformed by the states themselves (as we shall see). These characteristic deficiencies of the elected legislature were well-known to the framers of the state constitutions in the period between the Declaration and Constitution, which included Adams, Jefferson, Franklin, Dickinson, George Mason, and Robert Livingston. Their first American constitutions reflected the populist spirit of the Revolution in giving primacy to large elected legislatures, but they also included the first inklings of institutional constraints—bicameral legislatures, single executives, independent judiciaries, and bills of rights—hammered out by state conventions and written down for all to read, recite, and debate.[126]

Another frequent charge against the state legislatures was that they enacted protectionist commercial and transit laws that discriminated against citizens of other states and inhibited national development. However, almost all the proffered examples involved efforts of port states to discriminate against British shipping, turning the tables on Britain's prewar Navigation Acts.[127] Those measures led to rancorous interstate disputes over exempting imports bound for other states from port duties and restricting incoming traffic from other port states with lower or no such duties. The disputes were eventually settled through mutual agreement or at least détente—driven by the fact that the ports were competing with one another for traffic and revenue.[128]

The purely domestic commercial disputes, not involving foreign trade, mainly concerned interstate waterways. The most prominent, a dispute between Virginia and Maryland over the Potomac River, was resolved in three days at Washington's Mount Vernon estate in 1785 in an agreement covering navigation, tolls, fishing rights, and the financing of river improvements. Perversely, Madison, in his 1787 broadside, cited this "unlicensed compact" (meaning it was achieved at the state rather than national level) as one of the leading "vices of the political system of the United States."[129] Edmund W. Kitch, in his review of the state trade and tariff controversies of the 1780s, concludes:

> The theoretical arguments that decentralized authorities should be expected to cooperate to facilitate freedom of trade appear to be confirmed by the experience under the Articles of Confederation. The argument that this experience demonstrated the opposite is based on a misreading of the *Federalist* and it has no support in primary source materials.[130]

It remains to be said that state laws, then and forever after, often melded in-state commercial preferences, impositions on citizens of other states, tit for tat with laws of other states, and worthy domestic interests. Disentangling purposes and effects is problematic in all but the most egregious cases, and whether federal regulation or interstate policy competition is preferable is an open question.[131] (The same question arises in international trade policy.) The Constitution did not settle the matter unambiguously, leaving the Supreme Court to police interstate economic exploitation under a "dormant commerce clause" doctrine that has been unstable, unpredictable from case to case, and subject to endless academic debate.[132] The problem was not an artifact of the Articles of Confederation.

The Inheritance Realized. The Articles of Confederation gave the colonial-governments-turned-states—long the most powerful institutions in the nation, and now the most practiced[133]—a head start on constitution building. This was immediately apparent when the delegates gathered for the Philadelphia Convention in 1787. Madison arrived early, loaded for bear and intent on abolishing state sovereignty through two devices—a bicameral national legislature apportioned by state population in both chambers, and a summary national veto over all state laws. His plan, supported by Washington, Franklin, Hamilton, Wilson, and Gouverneur Morris, died in the opening weeks. Several of the less populous states, led by New Jersey and Delaware, were irreconcilably opposed, along with a few medium-sized states such as Maryland and Connecticut. For the rest of the convention, everyone knew that a new constitution, if it was to come into being, would be one of shared sovereignty and powerful states-as-states.[134]

In the final document, the states were equally represented by their own delegates in the Senate and were major players in elections for Congress and president. They were endowed with plenary powers independent of the national government, with specific prohibitions—states may not "coin Money, emit Bills of Credit, make any Thing but gold and silver Coin a Tender in Payment of Debts; [or] pass any Bill of Attainder, ex post facto

Law, or Law impairing the Obligation of Contract."[135] The national government was constrained by an enumeration of congressional powers and by the bicameralism and separation-of-powers architecture pioneered by the state constitutions. The supremacy, necessary and proper, and general welfare clauses would eventually facilitate enormous growth in federal power, but the potential was little anticipated at the time.

As the constitutional pieces were falling into place in Philadelphia, Madison (and others, including Washington and Hamilton) despaired of the result—a system of dual sovereignty, with some powers unique, some shared, and some ambiguous and contestable. But as Madison turned to advocating ratification in the *Federalist* and at the Virginia ratification convention, he "embraced the very ambiguity [he] had condemned as a fatal weakness of the Constitution as its central strength."[136] The profundity of his argument suggests that Madison was not merely making the best of the cards he'd been dealt. Rather, his experience in Philadelphia seems to have enlarged his thinking on the problem of self-government and its institutional correctives. His arguments may be found in three of his *Federalist* installments.

First, in *Federalist* 10, he lays out his celebrated argument that (1) the "instability, injustice, and confusion" of political factions is "sown in the nature of man" and cannot be cured without "destroying the liberty which is essential to its existence" and (2) the best way of ameliorating the problem is a republic with a "greater number of citizens, and a greater sphere of country." In such an extended nation, in contrast to the states under the Articles of Confederation, there will be a "greater variety of parties and interests," making it difficult to form effective legislative factions with uniform interests and internal cohesion.[137]

Second, in *Federalist* 39, he describes the Constitution's plan as being a "composition" of national and state government, each with sources of authority, operations, and jurisdictions that are distinct and independent in some respects and mixed and overlapping in others.[138]

Finally, in his great *Federalist* 51, Madison synthesizes his extended-republic and mixed-sovereignty arguments. He invokes the principle of

competition, with a nod to commercial competition: "[The] policy of supplying, by opposite and rival interests, the defect of better motives, might
be traced through the whole system of human affairs, private as well as
public." The principle is applied within the proposed national government
(as it had been, very imperfectly, in the state governments) by separating
the powers and sources of authority of the legislature, executive, and judiciary and giving each the means and motives to resist encroachments of
the others. But the proposed federalist system supplies an additional layer
of protective competition:

> The power surrendered by the people is first divided between
> two distinct governments, and then the portion allotted to
> each subdivided among distinct and separate departments.
> Hence a double security arises to the rights of the people. The
> different governments will control each other, at the same
> time that each will be controlled by itself.

And then came the crowning advantage: The federal structure per-
mits a more extended republic than would be possible under a unitary
national government and thereby a larger "variety of interests, parties,
and sects" to discourage the formation of oppressive national factions.
He concludes:

> The larger the society, provided it lie within a practicable
> sphere, the more duly capable it will be of self-government.
> And happily for the *republican cause*, the practicable sphere may
> be carried to a very great extent, by a judicious modification
> and mixture of the *federal principle*.[139] (Emphasis in original.)

Edward C. Banfield described the Constitution's federalism as "an accident"; although achieved through negotiation and accommodation, it was
less a product of "reason and choice" than of "competition and struggle."[140]
I would describe it, less pithily, as the institutionalization of inherited

circumstance. The constitutional provisions most associated with our founding capitalism—those forbidding impairment of contract and ex post facto laws and providing for a national currency, intellectual property rights, and an independent judiciary—were adaptations of British law and practice, adopted deliberately with little ado.[141] In contrast, federalism was homegrown and organic, no one's intention.[142] The decentralized political structure that had taken shape during the colonial period guided the Philadelphia Convention, which in turn bequeathed it to posterity.

The proposed Constitution corrected widely recognized deficiencies of state government and established an American national government in place of the British colonial government. During the ratification debates, the Anti-Federalists argued that the proposed national government, despite its republican foundations, limited powers, and structural constraints, would be as monarchal and abusive as Britain had been. Most citizens were apparently on the side of the Anti-Federalists (leave-us-alone revolutionary fervor was still running strong), but a sufficient majority of political leaders voted in the Constitution at the state conventions. Enterprising, entrepreneurial Americans contrived a scheme of government with rules and guidelines but no prescribed destination—a system that would depend on, and give ample opportunities to, the very qualities that brought it into being.

Competitive Pluralism in the New Republic

The extraordinary growth of the American economy after 1790 had multiple causes—the Constitution's protections of property and contract, the financial innovations of the Washington administration, and an enlarged spirit of "We the People" national destiny. It was also a period of cascading advances in transportation and manufacturing, science and technology, and literature and art that poured forth across the transatlantic world after 1815, when a long period of European and American wars subsided; Americans were in the avant-garde.[143]

Competitive pluralism, adumbrated at the beginning of this chapter, was integral to all these developments. It was an inheritance from the colonial period—the enterprising nature of the settlers and the diverse, self-governing circumstances of their settlements—that found new assignments in the new constitutional order.

Competition in political and economic affairs is different from tooth-and-claw biological competition. It is a means of directing self-seeking human beings toward cooperation with others for a larger common good (although many will enjoy the competition for its own sake). For this, it requires generally accepted rules of conduct, a degree of moral character in the participants, and an organizing structure. The rules of American competition are set forth in federal and state constitutions (such as the rule against ex post facto laws), common law and political tradition (such as rules of contract and against fraud and coercion), and statutes (such as rules for organizing corporations). Moral character is not, in America, prescribed by secular authorities, but the leading founders understood it to be essential; they preached it earnestly and often exemplified it.

Our organizing structure, since 1788, has been the Constitution's structure of government. In the remainder of this chapter, we shall examine the role of that structure in early America's energetic plunge into modern finance and the subsequent, equally energetic emergence of state-based national development.

The importance of structure is immediately apparent in the capitalist Big Bang of the early 1790s—the infant government's assumption of state and confederation war debts, creation of a national currency and national securities markets, and chartering of the Bank of the United States (BUS). These brilliant, hugely successful measures were largely the work of one man, Secretary of the Treasury Hamilton, with the strong and politically adroit support of President Washington. They would never have been adopted by Congress on its own, nor by a parliamentary government (with the president a subordinate of Congress) such as that proposed by Madison at Philadelphia along with his other doomed initiatives.

Political sentiment in Congress was for letting the debts of the old regime discretely default and starting afresh with an unburdened federal government; few legislators understood the utility of debt assumption in establishing the government's authority and creditworthiness, and many were deeply suspicious of banks and finance. Congress wanted a national currency, and might have embraced Hamilton's specie standard, as Massachusetts had done in the late colonial period. But fiat money had its advocates, and Congress would not have emitted money of any sort through the complex machinations of a national bank whose advantages took some explaining.

The adoption of the financial program was the first vindication of the framers' invention of an "energetic" single executive with his own electoral mandate independent of Congress. Separation of powers within the national government was for balancing as well as checking. The three branches were designed to specialize in distinctive political functions— the Congress in representation and deliberation, the executive in action and leadership, and the judiciary in principled dispute resolution.[144] Hamilton, like Washington, was a man of strong executive temperament, one who recognized the necessity of representation and deliberation but found them exasperating in practice. (Madison, by contrast, was a skillful legislator but a dithering, ineffective president.)

The constitutional structure obliges Congress to contend with a coequal personage whose inclinations are independent of, and often contrary to, those of its own councils and leadership. The results have been strong and durable, with a big assist from our federalist structure. In parliamentary systems (and some foreign presidential systems), the head of government is chosen from the national legislative establishment. In the United States since 1828, when Andrew Jackson brought our era of founder-presidents to a dramatic close, only four of our 34 elected presidents have come directly from Congress (all from the Senate).[145] Half of them—10 governors and seven military leaders—have been men of demonstrated executive ability. Every few decades, the new president is a determined political entrepreneur bent on overturning an ossified

Washington consensus—Jackson, Lincoln, Theodore Roosevelt, FDR, Reagan, and Donald Trump.

Hamilton's financial program was nationalist but not unitary—it depended on, and fostered, political and economic competition. The nationalization of state debts was a sweet spot in federal-state specialization. The new federal government used the debt to establish good credit for financing regular operations and future contingencies, plus a national currency and securities markets to capitalize the private economy. At the same time, the states were launched on new development ventures, from transportation to schools to manufacturing, freed from the bleak options of defaulting on debts or raising taxes for redemption. The national mint, specie standard, and dollar metric gave producers, consumers, and investors a uniform unit of account and stable, noninflationary currency.

The BUS was largely private—80 percent of its $10 million ownership capital was purchased by private (including some foreign) investors, the other 20 percent by the United States.[146] Unlike the colonial proto-banks, the BUS was full-service: It could issue bills of credit (convertible into specie) that served as currency, take deposits (with checking features), and make loans. Its primary customer for these services was the federal government, but other customers included private investors, business corporations (to whom it could make direct loans), and state banks. With a growing network of branches, the BUS made for expeditious commercial and government remittances across the nation.

But the BUS had nothing like the monopoly position of the Bank of England. In Britain, private banks were limited to small family partnerships, but in America they were corporations, propelled by interstate competition. The Constitution forbade states from coining money, emitting bills of credit, or making anything but gold and silver coin legal tender—but said nothing about banks. States immediately seized the opportunity to charter full-service banks, modeled on the BUS and intended to attune finance to state and local interests. These banks made loans to state governments and businesses, took deposits from both, and issued convertible bills of credit in small denominations suitable for everyday currency. Like the BUS, they were often owned in part by their state governments (in a few cases, fully owned) and paid dividends that were important sources of state revenue.

State-chartered banks numbered only three in 1790 but grew to 28 in 1800, 102 in 1810, 327 in 1820, and many more thereafter. The ownership capital of the state banks quickly surpassed the BUS capitalization of $10 million—totaling $17 million in 1800, $56 million in 1810, and $160 million in 1820. As best we can tell, the value of state banknotes circulating as money exceeded the sum of BUS notes and US Mint coins by 1800.

The construction of this system involved a remarkable degree of entrepreneurship. The specie standard, intended to supplant unstable fiat money, was highly aspirational. The United States was no longer being drained of specie by British mercantilism, and began accumulating gold and silver from foreign trade, foreign loans, and domestic mining. But the accumulation was slow. The US Mint was able to produce a measly $2.5 million in gold and silver coins throughout the 1790s (Martha Washington contributed some of her silverware for the project), and foreign coins predominated well into the 19th century. No one expected banknotes to be matched one-to-one by specie reserves—but the customary standard of one-to-five was little inquired into, and notes in circulation greatly exceeded available specie and were growing at a much higher rate.

Under the circumstances, government and private finance remained grounded ultimately on debt and land, just as in the colonial period. In other words, they remained grounded on confidence in the nation's future. Holders of federal debt instruments could use them as security for personal and commercial loans. Owners of state banks, including state governments, had some liability for redeeming notes and deposits beyond available specie, and in a pinch the BUS might help out, as it did on a few occasions in the early 1790s. The federal debt was on a schedule of interest and redemption payments attached to a sinking fund of tax revenues—but if the revenues failed to materialize, there was always the backstop of land sales, which were pledged exclusively to debt retirement.

That never came to pass, and early land sales were meager for reasons I have noted, but the latent treasure of undeveloped land was strong assurance of a growing economy and growing federal revenues.

The implicit growth strategy worked. The complex arithmetic of Hamilton's program of debt assumption and repayment concealed an inconvenient fact—that redemption would require revenues greatly in excess of any reasonable projections of receipts from federal duties on imports and vessels. In his first year as Treasury secretary, Hamilton had to borrow new money to cover interest payments and meet payroll for Congress and executive officials, and he floated the idea of suspending interest payments to some debt holders. But then revenues boomed—growing 26 percent annually from 1790 to 1795, from $1.6 million to $6.1 million, and then to $10.8 million in 1800. Economist Richard Sylla writes:

> The upsurge in revenue was due in good part to a higher real rate of economic growth along with a rising price level that resulted from monetary expansion rooted in both domestic (bank expansion) and foreign (capital inflows as foreign investors purchased American securities) sources....
>
> ... Economic growth ratified the risky bets on the future of entrepreneurs. In the early 1790s, the main entrepreneur was the secretary of the treasury, who bet that his comprehensive program of financial innovation and reform would jump-start economic growth and make it possible for the federal government to pay much more interest on its debt than seemed possible when the decisions were made to make those payments in 1790.[147]

Improvisation also paid off handsomely at the BUS. The bank's initial capitalization of $10 million was required by statute to include $2 million in specie (the one-to-five standard)—but it was permitted to begin operations when $400,000 in specie had come in, and apparently little or no more than that ever arrived. The government's $2 million capital contribution was legerdemain: The Treasury borrowed $2 million from the BUS itself to purchase its shares, promising to repay the loan from future dividends on those shares. And the BUS prospered. Bray Hammond, in his prodigious *Banks and Politics in America* (winner of the 1958 Pulitzer Prize for History), is more than forgiving:

> The early Americans were short of capital, particularly capital in the form of gold and silver. If that dearth of gold and silver had been allowed to hold up their formation of banks, the circle would never have been broken; instead they resorted to arrangements which had the practical virtue of establishing the proper procedure in principle if not in fact. And in time, because the pretense worked, they accumulated the gold and silver and made the principle a reality. . . . For the most part a saner and more honest practice in capitalization established itself as soon as a surplus of wealth made it possible. Without the initial act of faith, so to speak, the surplus would have been slower in coming. The Americans had declared their political independence before it was a reality, not after; and what they did in the matter of financial competence was much the same.[148]

The new financial system also featured corruption of both the hard and soft variety. By hard corruption, I mean bribery, kickbacks, and inside dealing, and there were certainly many instances at the state level. (Hamilton himself was spotless, and survived many inquiries into his financial stewardship and dealings with wealthy Federalist investors.) By soft corruption, I mean properly enacted laws that profit "special interests" at the expense of the general public—a larger and more important phenomenon. In America's early decades, corporate charters were granted by state legislation to specific individuals for specific purposes; these individuals were often politically well-connected, and the grants often included commercial privileges of one kind or another. Banks were in a class of their own because they were in continuous partnership with the states that chartered them. The states were usually major owners of the banks and thereby recipients of dividends on their earnings, giving them a joint interest with the private owners in the banks' profitability. And bank chartering process was the occasion for securing special state privileges, such as preferential interest rates on loans and charges on deposits.

As a result, states tightly restricted entry into banking, imposed geographic restrictions on their operations, and excluded out-of-state banks, all for the purpose of generating monopoly pricing power. The 28 state banks that had formed by 1800 included only two apiece in the nation's largest cities: Philadelphia, New York, Boston, and Baltimore. The BUS branches in those cities and a few others provided some competition, but it is fair to characterize the early banking system as one of "segmented monopolies."[149]

Federalism proved to be a powerful engine of creative monopoly destruction. The states were competing intensely for population and economic development, expanding the voting franchise for that purpose (eliminating property requirements, among other things). That changed the political dynamics of state legislatures, which became more attentive to demands for expanded credit and other banking services. At the same time, the federal government was proving ineffective at nation building.[150] The need for new canals, roads, turnpikes, and bridges was manifest, but federal revenues were dedicated largely to servicing the debt. In Congress, development initiatives invariably favored some states and regions at the expense of others—which defeated efforts to build coalitions for new taxing and spending. Moreover, many in the ascendant Republican Party opposed the initiatives on constitutional grounds.

The states moved into the vacuum with gusto, initiating ambitious transportation and development projects of their own that required heavy borrowing and more local banks. Between 1790 and 1860, the federal government spent only $60 million on transportation improvements (mostly scattered lighthouses and river-and-harbor projects), while the states spent more than $450 million. Westward development was driven by competition among states, regions, and private enterprises, not national planning.

Financial historians Charles W. Calomiris and Stephen H. Haber explain:

> Political competition within and among states undermined the incentives of state legislatures to constrain the number of charters they granted. Massachusetts began to increase the number of charters it granted as early as 1812, abandoning its strategy of holding bank stock as a source of state finance and instead levying taxes on bank stock. Pennsylvania followed with the Omnibus Banking Act of 1814.[151]

The result was the tenfold expansion of state banks in 20 years, from 28 in 1800 to 327 in 1820.

The federal government's constitutional reluctance to finance national development points to another impetus behind competitive state banking. This was the rise of Jefferson's Republicans in the early 1800s, as Hamilton's Federalists declined from national leadership to regional irrelevance following his death.[152] Jefferson and his followers were profoundly attached to the simplicity and connectedness of agrarian life and loathed big government and high finance. They were not, however, averse to commerce and trade so long as these were centered on the needs of farming and agriculture. Jefferson himself had orchestrated Virginia's abolition of primogeniture and entail in the mid-1770s—an extension of the colonial-era legal reforms in converting land from aristocratic bulwark to democratic asset—which most other states followed. As president, he touted more and better domestic manufacturing—always noting that it should be "household" manufacturing of "coarse and middling" family goods.[153]

Moreover, Jefferson and his party were avid for territorial expansion and westward migration. Agrarian development of the west was seen as a virtuous republican alternative to Hamilton's "consolidated" development of the urbanized Eastern Seaboard. Jefferson authored the Land

Ordinance of 1784 and Northwest Ordinance of 1787, sent the Lewis and Clark Expedition to the Pacific coast in 1804–06, and regarded the Louisiana Purchase as the crowning achievement of his presidency. In 1806, he proposed a national development program of "public education, roads, rivers, [and] canals" (which went nowhere—he thought it required a constitutional amendment).[154] His secretary of the Treasury, Albert Gallatin, was as expansion minded as Jefferson and nearly as financially sophisticated as Hamilton. Gallatin convinced the president to support (reluctantly) the BUS and demonstrated its utility in the Louisiana Purchase (largely debt financed) and other measures. Jefferson's Republican successor, Madison, unwisely permitted the BUS charter to lapse in 1811—and then, following the hard lessons of the financially starved War of 1812, presided over the chartering of the Second Bank of the United States in 1816 with strong Republican support.

The demands of national leadership moved the Republicans in a more practical direction, as did the party's growing political success and increasingly democratic followership. Jefferson historian Drew R. McCoy observes:

> The Republican party attracted political support from . . . Americans whose outlook can properly be termed entrepreneurial. Opposition to the Federalist system was never limited to agrarian-minded ideologues who unequivocally opposed a dynamic commercial economy. Many Jeffersonians were anxious to participate in the creation of an expansive economy and to reap its many rewards. . . . Ambitious men-on-the-make, engaged in a variety of economic pursuits, enlisted under the banner of Jeffersonianism in a crusade to secure the advantages and opportunities they desired.[155]

These developments illustrate the dynamic interplay of competition among states, between the federal and state governments, and between political parties. The structure of the emerging two-party system pointed political competition toward the electoral middle; ideology could not reign supreme but had to work alongside the necessities of party recruitment and victory in two-candidate races, plus the practical record of office holding in the face of outrageous fortune. The decommissioning of the First Bank of the United States was engineered by a coalition of "Old Republicans" opposed to the bank on constitutional and philosophical grounds, "New Republicans" intent on national development requiring profuse credit, and local entrepreneurs hoping to launch their own banks free of BUS competition and oversight. When the BUS lapsed, its eight branches were immediately purchased by local investors and chartered as state banks, followed by hundreds more across the country—whose founders assured state legislators of their fidelity to the Republican cause.

Similar events surrounded President Jackson's termination of the Second Bank of the United States, achieved through years of maneuvering against the bank's president, Nicholas Biddle, and vetoing of Biddle's bank reauthorization bill in 1832, leading to the bank's closure when its federal charter lapsed in 1836. Jackson was a hard-money man, opposed to debt of all varieties; many of his Democratic Party enlistees were neither of those—but shared his antipathy to centralized federal finance. Hammond writes that the Second Bank

> was not destroyed by the champions of the helpless contending against the money power, but by a rising and popular business interest that found the Bank doubly offensive for being both vested and regulatory—Wall Street, the state banks, and speculative borrowers dressing up for the occasion in the rags of the poor and parading with outcries of oppression by the aristocratic Mr. Biddle's hydra of corruption, whose nest they aspired to occupy themselves.[156]

The Second Bank of the United States was seamlessly rechartered as the United States Bank of Pennsylvania, with the identical management (including Biddle) and directors (other than ex officio Secretary of the

Treasury Roger B. Taney) and a similarly august name. Some federal deposits and other business stayed with the "United States Bank," but most were transferred to "pet banks" with prominent Democratic investors. (An example of the tightness of government and finance in those days is that Secretary Taney was an investor in one of the state banks that received the public funds.) By 1840, the number of state banks doubled to 901 with outstanding loans of $463 million; in 1860, there were 1,562 state banks with $692 million outstanding.[157] Increasingly, loan portfolios diversified from territorial development (land and transportation) to business development (agriculture, manufacturing, and merchandising), much of it highly speculative.

Lightly regulated, pro-growth, nation-building state banking was not a model of rock-solid financial stability. The closures of the First and Second Banks of the United States eliminated a stable benchmark national currency and some regulation of the soundness of state banks, and they were followed by periods of inflation and easy credit that led to painful contractions and the failure of many state banks (especially those with heavy state ownership). The state banks were part and parcel of the pell-mell territorial development that produced spectacular successes (the Erie Canal was profitable before it was completed and reduced the price of export-bound goods in New York City by a factor of 10) but equally spectacular overborrowing that led to a cascade of state defaults in the 1839–43 financial panic and ensuing economic depression.[158] Among the state bank bankruptcies was Pennsylvania's United States Bank, in 1841.

But competitive pluralism proved to be an excellent teacher and reformer, as it had been during the colonial period of fiat currency. The most important reform was "free banking," part of a larger movement that abolished case-by-case legislative chartering of corporations with its attendant crony capitalism and special privileges.[159] Under free banking and other laws, investors could establish a bank (or other business) as a limited liability corporation without permission from the legislature— simply by filing the attendant paperwork and observing specified requirements concerning capitalization, voting rules, and other matters. Many states conditioned bond issuances on voter-approved taxes to service the bonds. Competition from the federal government returned in the National Bank Acts of 1863 and 1865, which established a new network of national banks chartered on free-banking principles but with higher capital standards than most state banks. The national banks were required to redeem each other's notes at par; this, along with a discriminatory tax on state bank notes, reestablished something of a national currency, and encouraged state banks to concentrate on lending and deposit-taking.

These measures did not eliminate all political impositions on banking. Many states continued to limit banks to a single location rather than permitting them to establish branches in multiple locations. Banks in these "unit banking" states tended to charge higher interest rates on loans, reflecting limited local competition, while being less stable and more prone to failure, reflecting lower loan diversification than banks with multiple branches.[160] But unit banks had the virtue, especially important in farming communities, of sticking with their local customers through poor harvests and other hard times, when far-off city branch bankers—stable and diversified but personally detached—would unhesitatingly foreclose.

The great strength of the state-led financial structure was a diversity of banking and development arrangements that suited the nation's tremendous variety of population, demography, culture, climate, natural resources, and forms of agriculture, industry, and trade.[161] Economists Peter Rousseau and Richard Sylla conclude:

> The early Americans did not invent the banking corporation, but as of 1790 the world had seen few examples of it, and these were privileged monopolies such as the Bank of England. What the Americans did, uniquely when they did it, was charter so many banking corporations that they had to compete with one another rather than enjoy monopolistic privileges. From the 1790s to the middle of the nineteenth century, nowhere else in the world was the banking corporation as a competitive business enterprise developed to the extent that it was in the United

States. Only then, six or seven decades after the American innovation, did the old nations of the world begin to emulate the United States by allowing competitive corporate banking.[162]

By 1888, the 100th anniversary of the Constitution's ratification and first national elections, the United States spanned a vast continent and had become the world's largest economy and greatest industrial power. The colonial and founding bequests of political and economic competition were fundamental causes of this preeminence. Americans may or may not have understood the sources of their stupendous prosperity, but it was now theirs to enjoy, employ, and contend with in a looming new era.

Notes

1. Robert A. Goldwin and William A. Schambra, eds., *How Capitalistic Is the Constitution?* (Washington, DC: AEI Press, 1982), https://www.aei.org/research-products/book/how-capitalistic-is-the-constitution.

2. Karl Marx, *Capital: A Critique of Political Economy*, trans. Ben Fowkes and David Fernbach, vols. 1–3 (1867, 1885, 1894; London: Penguin Classics, 1992–93); and Milton Friedman, *Capitalism and Freedom* (Chicago: University of Chicago Press, 1962).

3. Thomas Piketty, *Capital in the Twenty-First Century*, trans. Arthur Goldhammer (Cambridge, MA: Harvard University Press, 2014).

4. For excellent expositions, see Jonathan Levy, *Ages of American Capitalism: A History of the United States* (New York: Random House, 2021), xiii–xxviii; and James Fulcher, *Capitalism: A Very Short Introduction* (Oxford, UK: Oxford University Press, 2004), 1–18. An extended treatment is Geoffrey M. Hodgson, *Conceptualizing Capitalism: Institutions, Evolution, Future* (Chicago: University of Chicago Press, 2015).

5. My views overlap broadly with those of Marc F. Plattner, Forrest McDonald, and Bernard H. Siegan in Goldwin and Schambra, eds., *How Capitalistic Is the Constitution?*, chaps. 1, 3, and 5. However, I depart sharply from McDonald's argument that the colonial economy at the time of the founding was dominated by agrarian, precapitalist norms. (My arguments are based largely on research that has appeared since his essay.)

6. James W. Ely Jr., *The Guardian of Every Other Right: A Constitutional History of Property Rights*, 3rd ed. (New York: Oxford University Press, 2008); and Paul J. Larkin Jr., "The Original Understanding of 'Property' in the Constitution," *Marquette Law Review* 100 (2016): 1–80, http://scholarship.law.marquette.edu/mulr/vol100/iss1/2.

7. Joseph E. Stiglitz, *People, Power, and Profits: Progressive Capitalism for an Age of Discontent* (New York: W. W. Norton, 2019).

8. Christopher DeMuth, "How Entitlements Ate Our Future: From Balanced Budgets to Borrowed Benefits," *Coolidge Review*, July 15, 2024, 29, https://www.coolidgereview.com/articles/how-entitlements-ate-our-future.

9. Naomi R. Lamoreaux and John Joseph Wallis, "Economic Crisis, General Laws, and the Mid-Nineteenth-Century Transformation of American Political Economy," *Journal of the Early Republic* 41, no. 3 (Fall 2021): 403–33, https://dx.doi.org/10.1353/jer.2021.0054.

10. Thomas K. McCraw, *The Founders and Finance: How Hamilton, Gallatin, and Other Immigrants Forged a New Economy* (Cambridge, MA: Belknap Press, 2012), 97–121; Ron Chernow, *Alexander Hamilton* (New York: Penguin Books, 2004), 295–357; Forrest McDonald, "The Constitution and Hamiltonian Capitalism," in Goldwin and Schambra, *How Capitalistic Is the Constitution?*, 68–71; and Forrest McDonald, *Alexander Hamilton: A Biography* (New York: W. W. Norton, 1982), 163–227.

11. Chernow, *Alexander Hamilton*, 275.

12. The philosophical agreements are elaborated in Thomas G. West, *The Political Theory of the American Founding: Natural Rights, Public Policy, and the Moral Conditions of Freedom* (Cambridge, UK: Cambridge University Press, 2017); and Thomas G. West, "The Economic Principles of America's Founders: Property Rights, Free Markets, and Sound Money," Heritage Foundation, August 30, 2010, https://www.heritage.org/political-process/report/the-economic-principles-americas-founders-property-rights-free-markets-and. The practical disagreements are elaborated in Michael J. Klarman, *The Framers' Coup: The Making of the United States Constitution* (New York: Oxford University Press, 2016).

13. "New Pluralists" promote the American "promise of pluralism—people of varied backgrounds and beliefs building community, finding belonging, and drawing on their differences to solve shared problems." See New Pluralists, "Many Voices, One Future: Building a Nation of Belonging for All," https://newpluralists.org. William A. Galston examines the virtues and problems of this vision in William A. Galston, *Liberal Pluralism: The Implications of Value Pluralism for Political Theory and Practice* (Cambridge, UK: Cambridge University Press, 2002); and William A. Galston, *The Practice of Liberal Pluralism* (Cambridge, UK: Cambridge University Press, 2005). Contemporary "post-liberals" such as Patrick J. Deneen see mainly problems and few virtues in liberal pluralism. See Patrick J. Deneen, *Why Liberalism Failed* (New Haven, CT: Yale University Press, 2018).

14. "E Pluribus Unum" was first proposed as a national motto in 1776 and was adopted and placed on the Great Seal of the United States by the Continental Congress in 1782. US Department of State, Bureau of Public Affairs, "The Great Seal of the United States," July 2003, https://2009-2017.state.gov/documents/organization/27807.pdf. The motto began appearing on state currency in 1786 and on national currency in 1795. It is one of many examples of the melding of individualism and communitarianism

in America's founding politics; see Christopher DeMuth, "What American Conservatism Exists to Conserve," *Quadrant* 66, no. 11 (November 2022): 43–47.

15. America's mother country was "England" during the first colonial century and "Great Britain" following the Acts of Union of 1707. For convenience, I am generally using "Britain" and "British" throughout, a conventional practice.

16. Leading contemporary expositions are Lawrence M. Mead, *Burdens of Freedom: Cultural Difference and American Power* (New York: Encounter Books, 2019); Lawrence E. Harrison and Samuel P. Huntington, eds., *Culture Matters: How Values Shape Human Progress* (New York: Basic Books, 2000); and David S. Landes, *The Wealth and Poverty of Nations: Why Some Are So Rich and Some So Poor* (New York: W. W. Norton, 1998). The classic forerunner is Edward C. Banfield, *The Moral Basis of a Backward Society* (New York: Free Press, 1958).

17. Douglas C. North, *Institutions, Institutional Change and Economic Performance* (Cambridge, UK: Cambridge University Press, 1990); Daron Acemoglu, Simon Johnson, and James A. Robinson, "Institutions as a Fundamental Cause of Long-Run Growth," in *Handbook of Economic Growth*, ed. Philippe Aghion and Steven N. Durlauf (Amsterdam: North-Holland, 2005), chap. 6; and Hernando de Soto, *The Mystery of Capital: Why Capitalism Triumphs in the West and Fails Everywhere Else* (New York: Basic Books, 2000). A good précis of the debate is Michael Novak, "Is It Bad Culture or Bad Laws That Keep Some Countries Poor?," American Enterprise Institute, January 15, 2001, https://www.aei.org/articles/is-it-bad-culture-or-bad-laws-that-keep-some-countries-poor.

18. Samuel Huntington, "One Nation, Out of Many," *American Enterprise* 15, no. 6 (2004): 20, https://www.aei.org/articles/one-nation-out-of-many/. See also Samuel Huntington, *Who Are We? The Challenges to America's National Identity* (New York: Simon & Schuster, 2004), 59–105.

19. David Hackett Fischer, *Albion's Seed: Four British Folkways in America* (New York: Oxford University Press, 1989).

20. In addition to the sources specifically cited, this section draws on Levy, *Ages of American Capitalism*; Alan Greenspan and Adrian Wooldridge, *Capitalism in America: A History* (New York: Penguin Press, 2018); Sven Beckert and Christine Desan, eds., *American Capitalism: New Histories* (New York: Columbia University Press, 2018); Bhu Srinivasan, *Americana: A 400-Year History of American Capitalism* (New York: Penguin Press, 2017); John Steele Gordon, *An Empire of Wealth: The Epic History of American Economic Power* (New York: Harper Collins, 2004); John J. McCusker and Russell R. Menard, *The Economy of British America, 1607–1789* (Chapel Hill, NC: University of North Carolina Press, 1985); and George L. Priest, "The Capitalist Foundations of America," American Enterprise Institute, May 14, 2007, https://www.aei.org/research-products/speech/the-capitalist-foundations-of-America.

21. Alexis de Tocqueville, *Democracy in America*, trans. Harvey C. Mansfield and Delba Winthrop (Chicago: University of Chicago Press, 2000), 279.

22. Carl N. Degler, *Out of Our Past: The Forces That Shaped Modern America*, 3rd ed. (1959; New York: Harper Perennial, 1984), 2. Carl Degler's aphorism was criticized by later historians who argued that the early settler-farmers were more communitarian than capitalist. But he was making a different point—that the settlers were attracted to the colonies by the abundance of land and scarcity of labor (the opposite of conditions in England and the Netherlands) and that those conditions fostered the rise of farmers and other working people in wealth, social status, and political influence. The point is elaborated in the text at page 123.

23. Edwin J. Perkins, "The Entrepreneurial Spirit in Colonial America: The Foundations of Modern Business History," *Business History Review* 63, no. 1 (Spring 1989): 160–86, https://www.cambridge.org/core/journals/business-history-review/article/abs/entrepreneurial-spirit-in-colonial-america-the-foundations-of-modern-business-history/580A329B3BCBEC919E56DBD2052330A5; and Stephen Innis, ed., *Work and Labor in Early America* (Chapel Hill, NC: University of North Carolina Press, 1988). North America–bound indentured servants appear to have been selected, by their brokers and employers and by themselves, for "ability, motivation, ambition, physical strength and health." Ran Abramitzky and Fabio Braggion, "Migration and Human Capital: Self-Selection of Indentured Servants to the Americas," *Journal of Economic History* 66, no. 4 (December 2006): 882, 900, https://doi.org/10.1017/S0022050706000362.

24. Gordon S. Wood, "The Enemy Is Us: Democratic Capitalism in the Early Republic," *Journal of the Early Republic* 16, no. 2 (Summer 1996): 293–308, https://doi.org/10.2307/3124251; and Gordon S. Wood, "Inventing American Capitalism," *New York Review of Books*, June 9, 1994, https://www.nybooks.com/articles/1994/06/09/inventing-american-capitalism. The essays adjudicate the arguments of "moral economy historians," who emphasize the communitarian ethos of colonial New England farmers, and "market economy historians," who emphasize the growing integration of farm economies with larger commercial markets in the 18th century. An important subsequent contribution to this literature is Naomi R. Lamoreaux, "Rethinking the Transition to Capitalism in the Early American Northeast," *Journal of American History* 90, no. 2 (September 2003): 437–61, https://doi.org/10.2307/3659440. She finds that farmers, merchants, and manufacturers were similarly (1) alert to economic circumstances and opportunities and (2) reliant on family members and attentive to community norms.

25. Max Weber, *The Protestant Ethic and the Spirit of Capitalism*, trans. Talcott Parsons (Boston, MA: Allen and Unwin, 1930). The discussion in this section draws in several particulars on the superb studies of Benjamin M. Friedman, *Religion and the Rise of Capitalism* (New York: Knopf, 2021), 169–96, 228–62; and and Mark Valeri, *Heavenly Merchandize: How Religion Shaped Commerce in Puritan America* (Princeton, NJ: Princeton University Press, 2010).

26. The author's surname ancestors were Czech-Bohemian religious refugees brought to the colonies by James Oglethorpe and Nicolas Zinzendorf. They founded Bethlehem, Pennsylvania, as a Moravian Brethren missionary community in 1741. But the Demuths were also farmers, artisans, and merchants and helped convert

Bethlehem from a "communal economy" into a market economy in the 1760s. One of them, Christopher, established Demuth's Tobacco Shop in Lancaster, Pennsylvania, in 1770 and became a prominent businessman and real estate investor (and, despite Moravian pacifism, kept a rifle and joined the Pennsylvania militia in the Revolutionary War). "America's First Tobacco Shop" manufactured its own brand-name snuff and pipe tobacco in its nearby mill, expanded into wholesaling with credit and transportation services across the mid-Atlantic colonies, and was owned and managed by family descendants through 1986 (with the author among its latter-day cigar customers). A biographer notes that Demuth "benefitted from observing the entrepreneurial attitude of the Bethlehem elders in reaching out to non-Moravian customers and realizing profits, and he emulated this behavior when he went into business for himself." Diane Wenger, "Christopher Demuth: From 'Single Brother' to Celebrated Snuff Maker," *Pennsylvania Magazine of History and Biography* 141, no. 2 (April 2017): 115–44, https://doi.org/10.5215/pennmaghistbio.141.2.0115.

27. Gordon, *An Empire of Wealth*, 39.

28. The Puritans played a central role in the colonial innovation of government-issued currency, recounted in astonishing detail in Dror Goldberg, *Easy Money: American Puritans and the Invention of Modern Currency* (Chicago: University of Chicago Press, 2023). In particular, Cotton Mather was an influential advocate of paper money, publishing a widely read pamphlet on the subject in 1691, when Massachusetts had just issued its first "bills of credit" that were beginning to circulate as money (discussed later in this essay). That was shortly before Mather's equally influential pamphlet justifying the Salem witch trials of 1692.

29. Friedman, *Religion and the Rise of Capitalism*, 239–40.

30. Wood, "The Enemy Is Us," 307.

31. Roger Finke, "Religious Deregulation: Origins and Consequences," *Journal of Church and State* 32, no. 2 (Summer 1990): 609–26, https://doi.org/10.1093/jcs/32.3.60; and Peter L. Berger, "The Good of Religious Pluralism," *First Things*, April 2016, https://www.firstthings.com/article/2016/04/the-good-of-religious-pluralism.

32. Mark Häberlein, "Reform, Authority and Conflict in the Churches of the Middle Colonies, 1700–1770," in *Religious and Secular Reform in America: Ideas, Beliefs, and Social Change*, ed. David K. Adams and Cornelis A. van Minnen (New York: New York University Press, 1999), 20.

33. Tocqueville, *Democracy in America*, 280–83.

34. New Netherlands and its port city New Amsterdam (later New York City) were from their founding the most capitalist settlement in North America, supplying Puritan New England with valuable trade and instruction in Dutch commercial practices. Kim Todt, "Trading Between New Netherland and New England, 1624–1664," *Early American Studies* 9, no. 2 (Spring 2011): 348–78, https://dx.doi.org/10.1353/eam.2011.0018. And the neighboring Dutch colony provided all the British colonies with easy opportunities to evade Britain's mercantilist trade restrictions. Jonathan Barth, *The Currency of Empire: Money and Power in Seventeenth-Century English America* (Ithaca, NY: Cornell

University Press, 2021), 84–88, 114–16.

35. Claire Priest, *Credit Nation: Property Laws and Institutions in Early America* (Princeton, NJ: Princeton University Press, 2021), 21–37.

36. Deirdre Nansen McCloskey, *Bourgeois Equality: How Ideas, Not Capital or Institutions, Enriched the World* (Chicago: University of Chicago Press, 2016), 235–70.

37. Detailed in Bernard Bailyn, *The New England Merchants in the Seventeenth Century* (Cambridge, MA: Harvard University Press, 1955), 87–91.

38. Gordon, *An Empire of Wealth*, 14–20.

39. Colorfully recounted in Robert E. Pike, *Tall Trees, Tough Men* (New York: W. W. Norton, 1967), which begins, "It was the axe, even more than the rifle, that conquered the North American continent."

40. Pike, *Tall Trees, Tough Men*, 48.

41. Bailyn, *The New England Merchants in the Seventeenth Century*.

42. Bailyn, *The New England Merchants in the Seventeenth Century*, 61–74.

43. Bailyn, *The New England Merchants in the Seventeenth Century*, 1–15.

44. Bailyn, *The New England Merchants in the Seventeenth Century*, 38–39, 75, 169–70.

45. Bailyn, *The New England Merchants in the Seventeenth Century*, 34.

46. The account of this paragraph is drawn primarily from Jonathan Levy, *Freaks of Fortune: The Emerging World of Capitalism and Risk in America* (Cambridge, MA: Harvard University Press, 2012), 16–30.

47. Levy, *Freaks of Fortune*, 5.

48. Levy, *Freaks of Fortune*, 23–101.

49. Tocqueville, *Democracy in America*, 385–87.

50. Tocqueville, *Democracy in America*, 387.

51. Michael B. Oren, *Power, Faith, and Fantasy: America in the Middle East, 1776 to the Present* (New York: W. W. Norton, 2008), 18.

52. Degler, *Out of the Past*, 2.

53. Degler, *Out of the Past*, 2–3.

54. My account draws heavily on Priest, *Credit Nation*; De Soto, *The Mystery of Capital*, 105–51; and Amelia Clewley Ford, *Colonial Precedents of Our National Land System as It Existed in 1800*, University of Wisconsin, July 1910.

55. Priest, *Credit Nation*, 23.

56. Clewley Ford, *Colonial Precedents of Our National Land System as It Existed in 1800*, 83–102.

57. De Soto, *The Mystery of Capital*, 113–20.

58. De Soto, *The Mystery of Capital*, 119–20; and Clewley Ford, *Colonial Precedents of Our National Land System as It Existed in 1800*, 123–27.

59. Priest, *Credit Nation*, 38–56.

60. Priest, *Credit Nation*, 5. They were also controversial because recording fees and court fees were an important source of revenue, tussled over by local and colonial authorities.

61. Priest, *Credit Nation*, 59–111.

62. Priest, *Credit Nation*, 76–89.

63. Joseph Story, *Commentaries on the Constitution of the United States*, 3 vols. (Boston, MA: Hilliard, Gray, 1833), § 182, https://lonang.com/library/reference/story-commentaries-us-constitution/.

64. Priest, *Credit Nation*, 9, 150.

65. Story passes over the contributions of slavery to property reform, but Claire Priest examines them in unflinching detail.

66. Barth, *The Currency of Empire*, 23, 26. See also Levy, *Ages of American Capitalism*, 14–21.

67. Barth, *The Currency of Empire*, 95–98, 118–22, 167–77.

68. Barth, *The Currency of Empire*, 117, 134.

69. Claire Priest, "Currency Policies and Legal Development in Colonial New England," *Yale Law Journal* 110, no. 8 (June 2001): 1303, 1321–32, 1335–38, https://www.yalelawjournal.org/article/currency-policies-and-legal-development-in-colonial-new-england.

70. Priest, "Currency Policies and Legal Development in Colonial New England," 1331.

71. My account of colonial paper money draws on many excellent works: Barth, *The Currency of Empire*, 254–61; Goldberg, *Easy Money*, 131–41, 160–98; Peter L. Rousseau, "Monetary Policy and the Dollar," in *Founding Choices: American Economic Policy in the 1790s*, ed. Douglas A. Irwin and Richard Sylla (Chicago: University of Chicago Press, 2011), 121–49; James Macdonald, *A Free Nation Deep in Debt: The Financial Roots of Democracy* (Princeton, NJ: Princeton University Press, 2003), 277–89; Priest, "Currency Policies and Legal Development in Colonial New England," 1342–50, 1359–65, 1368–84; Leslie V. Brock, "The Colonial Currency, Prices, and Exchange Rates," *Essays in History* 34 (1992): 70–132, https://doi.org/10.25894/eih.464; Edwin J. Perkins, *The Economy of Colonial America*, 2nd. ed. (New York: Columbia University Press, 1988), 167–83; and Bray Hammond, *Banks and Politics in America from the Revolution to the Civil War* (Princeton, NJ: Princeton University Press, 1957), 3–39. For an online exposition and literature summary, see Ron Michener, "Money in the American Colonies," Economic History Association, January 13, 2011, https://eh.net/encyclopedia/money-in-the-american-colonies. I am mainly offering my own interpretation of these works, so I generally omit point-by-point citations.

72. Fiat paper money had been employed in China under the Yuan and Ming dynasties but was discontinued amid high inflation in the mid-1400s. There was some intermittent use of paper credits to pay soldiers during wartime in Britain, Europe, and Canada before 1690, but nothing on the scale that began (initially for the same purpose) in Massachusetts that year.

73. But they were really just brokers of currency for land, like the public land offices. Unlike modern banks, they had no capital of their own and did not take money deposits.

74. Detailed in Priest, "Currency Policies and Legal Development in Colonial New England," 1359–84. The value of Massachusetts bills fell by about 60 percent from 1720 until 1740 and then by another 50 percent from 1740 until 1750.

75. That was the view of several founders, of opponents of Williams Jennings Bryan and other populist champions of easy money in the late 19th century, and of hard-money advocates in our contemporary times of officially inflationary fiat money.

76. Modern economic scholarship agrees that the colonial economies were seriously under-monetized. Even in colonies with a well-managed official currency, a considerable volume of trade continued to be conducted by informal local arrangements. Rousseau, "Monetary Policy and the Dollar," 141–43.

77. Hammond, *Banks and Politics in America*, 12–35, shows that the most persistent and influential advocates of paper money were merchants and entrepreneurs, who understood the link between ample currency and economic growth. The most persistent and influential of them all was Benjamin Franklin, whose first broadside, "A Modest Enquiry into the Nature and Necessity of a Paper Currency," remains a classic. See Benjamin Franklin, "The Nature and Necessity of a Paper-Currency, 3 April 1729," Founders Online, https://founders.archives.gov/documents/Franklin/01-01-02-0041.

78. Successful adaptation is emphasized by Peter L. Rousseau, James Macdonald, Edwin J. Perkins, and Bray Hammond. Priest emphasizes the economic turmoil created by the sharp depreciation of Massachusetts notes, but her purpose is to show that commercial litigation in the 1700s was driven by that turmoil rather than expanding markets. See Priest, "Currency Policies and Legal Development in Colonial New England," 1355–59, 1384–404.

79. Christopher DeMuth, "The Rise and Rise of Deficit Government," Law & Liberty, May 5, 2021, https://lawliberty.org/the-rise-and-rise-of-deficit-government; and Christopher DeMuth, "Debt and Democracy," Legatum Institute, May 21, 2012, https://ccdemuth.com/debt-and-deficits/#toggle-id-10.

80. Macdonald's *A Free Nation Deep in Debt* is a comprehensive argument that the rise of debt financing in place of stored-up specie was integral to the rise of political democracy. The modern decline of public debt as a mechanism of currency stability and democratic accountability in the United States is detailed in Editors, "America in Debt: From Hamilton to the Fiscal Brink," *Coolidge Review*, July 9, 2024, https://www.coolidgereview.com/articles/america-in-debt.

81. One British misstep, in 1764 as the revolution in the colonies approached, was outlawing legal-tender requirements for both private and public obligations, a long-established monetary status of great symbolic importance to the colonists but probably of little practical importance. (Notes without it circulated widely.) When Franklin wisely advised the British that they could end the rancorous dispute by banning legal tender only for foreign transactions, they ignored him. Perkins, *The Economy of Colonial America*, 182–83.

82. For an ambitious historical account of the concurrent growth of government money and government power, see Christine Desan, *Making Money: Coin, Currency, and the Coming of Capitalism* (Oxford, UK: Oxford University Press, 2014).

83. Government financing by sale of investment-grade securities rather than emitting currency was a conventional practice in Britain and Europe by the 1700s.

Macdonald's *A Free Nation Deep in Debt* emphasizes the benefits of organized credit markets in disciplining government performance.

84. Joseph Ernst, *Money and Politics in America, 1755–1775: A Study in the Currency Act of 1764 and the Political Economy of Revolution* (Chapel Hill, NC: University of North Carolina Press, 1973). The British closing of the Massachusetts Land Bank in 1741 ruined Samuel Adams Sr., one of its founding subscribers, and inspired the entry of his son Sam Adams and cousin John Adams into revolutionary politics. Priest, "Currency Policies and Legal Development in Colonial New England," 1379–80.

85. Peter H. Lindert and Jeffrey G. Williamson, "American Colonial Incomes, 1650–1774," *Economic History Review* 69, no. 1 (February 2016): 54–77, https://doi.org/10.1111/ehr.12106; and Robert C. Allen, Tommy E. Murphy, and Eric B. Schneider, "The Colonial Origins of the Divergence in the Americas: A Labor Market Approach," *Journal of Economic History* 72, no. 4 (December 2012): 863–94, https://doi.org/10.1017/S0022050712000629. Robert Allen, Timothy Murphy, and Eric Schneider find that "for much of the seventeenth and eighteenth centuries, North America was the most prosperous region of the world, offering living standards at least as high as those in the booming parts of North-Western Europe. Latin America, on the other hand, was much poorer and offered a standard of living like that in Spain and less prosperous parts of the world in general."

86. Perkins, *The Economy of Colonial America*, 6–7, 212–17.

87. John Komlos, "On the Biological Standard of Living of Eighteenth-Century Americans: Taller, Richer, Healthier," *Research in Economic History* 20 (2001): 223–48, https://doi.org/10.1016/S0363-3268(01)20007-X; and Richard H. Steckel, "Stature and Living Standards in the United States," in *American Economic Growth and Standards of Living Before the Civil War*, ed. Robert A. Gallman and John Joseph Wallis (Chicago: University of Chicago Press, 1992), 265, 285–87, https://www.nber.org/system/files/chapters/c8012/c8012.pdf.

88. Perkins, *The Economy of Colonial America*, 1–14; and McCusker and Menard, *The Economy of British America*, 211–35.

89. S. D. Smith, "The Market for Manufactures in the Thirteen Continental Colonies, 1698–1776," *Economic History Review* 51, no. 4 (November 1998): 676–708, https://doi.org/10.1111/1468-0289.00110.

90. David Hackett Fischer, *Paul Revere's Ride* (Oxford, UK: Oxford University Press, 1994), 12–29, 138–64.

91. Rafael La Porta, Florencio Lopez-de-Silanes, and Andrei Shleifer, "The Economic Consequences of Legal Origins," *Journal of Economic Literature* 46, no. 2 (June 2008): 285–332, https://www.aeaweb.org/articles?id=10.1257/jel.46.2.285.

92. Allen, Murphy, and Schneider, "The Colonial Origins of the Divergence in the Americas."

93. Daron Acemoglu, Simon Johnson, and James A. Robinson, "The Colonial Origins of Comparative Development: An Empirical Investigation," *American Economic Review* 91, no. 5 (December 2001): 1369–401, https://www.aeaweb.org/articles?id=10.1257/aer.91.5.1369.

94. Stanley L. Engerman and Kenneth L. Sokoloff, *Economic Development in the Americas Since 1500: Endowments and Institutions* (Cambridge, UK: Cambridge University Press, 2012). Readers interested in exploring the origins literature should begin with this magnificent essay collection.

95. Daniel M. Klerman et al., "Legal Origin or Colonial History?," *Journal of Legal Analysis* 3 (2011): 379–409, https://ssrn.com/abstract=1903994.

96. See notes 16 and 17.

97. Vincent Geloso, "The Historical Evolution of Canadian Living Standards," *Oxford Research Encyclopedias, Economics and Finance*, June 20, 2020, https://doi.org/10.1093/acrefore/9780190625979.013.791; and Vincent Geloso, "Economic History of French Canadians," in *Handbook of Cliometrics*, ed. Claude Diebolt and Michael Haupert (New York: Springer, 2023), https://doi.org/10.1007/978-3-642-40458-0_107-1. An important reason for the poorer economic performance of French Canada appears to have been its institution of seigneurial tenure—a feudal remnant that restricted landownership, labor mobility, and other rights—that reigned in Quebec from 1626 through 1791 and continued in limited form until its abolition in 1854. See Vincent Geloso, Vadim Kufenko, and Alex P. Arsenault-Morin, "The Lesser Shades of Labor Coercion: The Impact of Seigneurial Tenure in Nineteenth-Century Quebec," *Journal of Development Economics* 163 (June 2023), https://doi.org/10.1016/j.jdeveco.2023.103091. Landownership was also highly concentrated in political elites in the Spanish colonies but through different mechanisms. See Gary D. Libecap, "The Consequences of Land Ownership," Hoover Institution, August 29, 2018, https://www.hoover.org/research/consequences-land-ownership.

98. Deirdre Nansen McCloskey, "Economic Causes and Consequences of the American Revolution," in *Capitalism and the American Revolution*, ed. Yuval Levin, Adam J. White, and John Yoo (Washington, DC: AEI Press, 2025).

99. Fischer, *Paul Revere's Ride*, 163–64.

100. Robert F. Smith, *Manufacturing Independence: Industrial Innovation in the American Revolution* (Yardley, PA: Westholme Publishing, 2016).

101. David Hackett Fischer, *Washington's Crossing* (New York: Oxford University Press, 2004), 11–12, 255–57, 264–66, 283–84, 310–16.

102. Doris Kearns Goodwin, *Team of Rivals: The Political Genius of Abraham Lincoln* (New York: Simon & Schuster, 2006); and David Hackett Fischer, "American Leadership: The Invention of a Tradition," American Enterprise Institute, March 8, 2006, https://www.c-span.org/video/?191737-1/irving-kristol-award.

103. F. A. Hayek, "Competition as a Discovery Procedure," trans. Marcellus S. Snow, *Quarterly Journal of Austrian Economics* 5, no. 3 (Fall 2002): 9–23, https://cdn.mises.org/qjae5_3_3.pdf.

104. McCusker and Menard, *The Economy of British America*.

105. Samuel H. Williamson, "Annualized Growth Rate of Various Historical Economic Series," MeasuringWorth, 2024, https://www.measuringworth.com/calculators/growth. See also Thomas Weiss, "Economic Growth in the United States, 1790–1860,"

Oxford Research Encyclopedias, Economics and Finance, December 23, 2019, https://doi.org/10.1093/acrefore/9780190625979.013.489. US economic growth continued at extraordinarily high rates after the Civil War.

106. Richard Sylla, "Financial Foundations: Public Credit, the National Bank, and Securities Markets," in Irwin and Sylla, *Founding Choices*, 59, 82–83.

107. Robert E. Wright, "Rise of the Corporation Nation," in Irwin and Sylla, *Founding Choices*, 217, Table 7-1.

108. Douglass C. North, *The Economic Growth of the United States: 1790–1860* (New York: W. W. Norton, 1966).

109. Wright, "Rise of the Corporation Nation," 219.

110. Empirical evidence that economic growth in the new republic's early decades was "finance led" is presented in Peter L. Rousseau and Richard Sylla, "Emerging Financial Markets and Early U.S. Growth," *Explorations in Economic History* 42, no. 1 (January 2005): 1–26, https://www.sciencedirect.com/science/article/abs/pii/S0014498304000178.

111. Mark F. Plattner, "American Democracy and the Acquisitive Spirit," in Goldwin and Schambra, eds., *How Capitalistic Is the Constitution?*, 1–2, 9. Essentially all the *Federalist*'s examples of the debilities of the Articles of Confederation and advantages of the proposed Constitution involve economic policy. Those in the central pair of James Madison's *Federalist* 10 and Alexander Hamilton's *Federalist* 11 are laws concerning debtors versus creditors, manufacturers versus landed interests, apportionment of taxes, and promotion of competition among foreign nations to secure favorable terms for American commerce. "The principal task of modern legislation," says *Federalist* 10, is regulation of these "various and interfering interests" and of the "unequal distribution of property," the protection of which is "the first object of government." See *Federalist*, no. 10 (James Madison), https://avalon.law.yale.edu/18th_century/fed10.asp.

112. National Archives, "Signers of the Declaration of Independence," https://www.archives.gov/founding-docs/signers-factsheet; and National Archives, "Meet the Framers of the Constitution," https://www.archives.gov/founding-docs/founding-fathers.

113. Three recent books examine George Washington's entrepreneurial exploits before and after the Revolutionary War and highlight his business skills and business-friendly policies as president: Edward G. Lengel, *First Entrepreneur: How George Washington Built His—and the Nation's—Prosperity* (Boston, MA: Da Capo Press, 2016); Cyrus A. Ansary, *George Washington, Dealmaker-in-Chief: The Story of How the Father of Our Country Unleashed the Entrepreneurial Spirit in America* (Washington, DC: Lambert Publications, 2019); and John Berlau, *George Washington, Entrepreneur: How Our Founding Father's Private Business Pursuits Changed America and the World* (New York: All Points Books, 2020).

114. I. Bernard Cohen, *Science and the Founding Fathers: Science in the Political Thought of Thomas Jefferson, Benjamin Franklin, John Adams, and James Madison* (New York: W. W. Norton, 1995). Jefferson was of course an architect; he also tried his hand at

business, organizing a for-profit nail factory atop Monticello in an effort to reduce his substantial personal debts, which ultimately failed despite being manned by slave labor.

115. R. R. Palmer, *Twelve Who Ruled: The Year of the Terror in the French Revolution* (1941; Princeton, NJ: Princeton University Press, 2017), 5–18. R. R. Palmer summarizes: "Not one of the twelve had ever labored with his hands. . . . None, . . . except Saint-André for a short time, had ever engaged in trade. They had no personal knowledge of industry. . . . All twelve were intellectuals." Hamilton wrote to the Marquis de Lafayette about the French revolutionaries in 1789: "I dread the reveries of your philosophic politicians who appear in the moment to have great influence and who being mere speculatists may aim at more refinement than suits either with human nature or the composition of your nation." Chernow, *Alexander Hamilton*, 318.

116. Irving Kristol, *The American Revolution as a Successful Revolution* (Washington, DC: American Enterprise Institute, 1973), https://www.aei.org/wp-content/uploads/2016/03/BicentenUSA01.pdf.

117. Peter H. Lindert and Jeffrey G. Williamson, "American Incomes Before and After the Revolution," *Journal of Economic History* 73, no. 3 (September 2013): 725–65, https://doi.org/10.1017/S0022050713000594.

118. Winifred Barr Rothenberg, *From Market-Places to a Market Economy: The Transformation of Rural Massachusetts, 1750–1850* (Chicago: University of Chicago Press, 1992).

119. Wood, "Inventing American Capitalism." This is drawing on the larger argument of Gordon S. Wood, *The Radicalism of the American Revolution* (New York: Knopf, 1991). A more recent assessment is Gordon S. Wood, *Power and Liberty: Constitutionalism in the American Revolution* (New York: Oxford University Press, 2021), 54–71.

120. Wright, "Rise of the Corporation Nation," 219.

121. *Federalist*, no. 7 (Alexander Hamilton); *Federalist*, no. 10 (Madison); *Federalist*, no. 11 (Alexander Hamilton); *Federalist*, no. 22 (Alexander Hamilton); and *Federalist*, no. 46 (James Madison).

122. James Madison, "Vices of the Political System of the United States, April 1797," Founders Online, https://founders.archives.gov/documents/Madison/01-09-02-0187.

123. Farley Grubb, "U.S. Land Policy: Founding Choices and Outcomes, 1781–1802," in Irwin and Sylla, *Founding Choices*, 259–66. Some complicated western claims were left for resolution under the Articles of Confederation.

124. "The Constitution was a conservative counterrevolution against what leading American statesmen regarded as the irresponsible economic measures enacted by a majority of state legislatures in the mid-1780s, which they diagnosed as a symptom of excessive democracy." Klarman, *The Founders' Coup*.

125. The Constitution forbade federal and state bills of attainder and ex post facto laws with the only, fleeting objections being that they were too obviously contrary to the legislative function to be worth mentioning and had already been banned by many state constitutions. US Const. art. I, § 9, cl. 3.1–3.2. See Constitution Annotated, "Historical Background on Bills of Attainder," https://constitution.congress.gov/browse/essay/artI-S9-C3-1/ALDE_00013186; and Constitution Annotated, "Historical

Background on Ex Post Facto Laws," https://constitution.congress.gov/browse/essay/artI-S9-C3-3-2/ALDE_00013191.

126. Wood, *Power and Liberty*, 32–53.

127. An exception was the treaty proposal of Secretary of Foreign Affairs John Jay that the confederation relinquish navigation rights on the Mississippi River for several decades in exchange for favorable trade arrangements with Spain. Madison, who was strongly opposed, regarded the jockeying for regional advantages in the treaty debates as a prime example of the "predominance of temporary and partial interests over those just and extended maxims of policy" under the articles. But those debates produced exactly the result he thought just—Congress rejected the treaty. See Joseph J. Ellis, *American Creation: Triumphs and Tragedies in the Founding of the Republic* (New York: Knopf, 2007), 95–96.

128. Edmund W. Kitch, "Regulation and the American Common Market," in *Regulation, Federalism, and Interstate Commerce*, ed. A. Dan Tarlock (Cambridge, MA: Oelgeschlager, Gunn & Hain, 1981), 9, 15–19.

129. Adams's one other lamentable "unlicensed compact" was a similarly businesslike 1783 agreement between Pennsylvania and New Jersey over navigation and trade on the Delaware River.

130. Kitch, "Regulation and the American Common Market," 19.

131. That is the question addressed in the Kitch essay and others in the Tarlock volume.

132. In addition to the Tarlock volume, see Michael S. Greve, *The Upside-Down Constitution* (Cambridge, MA: Harvard University Press, 2012); Robin Feldman and Gideon Schor, "Lochner Revenant: The Dormant Commerce Clause & Extraterritoriality," *New York University Journal of Law & Liberty* 16, no. 2 (2022): 209, https://repository.uclawsf.edu/cgi/viewcontent.cgi?article=2921&context=faculty_scholarship; Daniel Francis, "The Decline of the Dormant Commerce Clause," *Denver Law Review* 94, no. 2 (January 2017): 255, https://digitalcommons.du.edu/cgi/viewcontent.cgi?article=1043&context=dlr; and Norman R. Williams, "The Foundations of the American Common Market," *Notre Dame Law Review* 84, no. 1 (2008): 409, https://scholarship.law.nd.edu/ndlr/vol84/iss1/7/.

133. Elaborated in Aaron N. Coleman, *The American Revolution, State Sovereignty, and the American Constitutional Settlement, 1765–1800* (Lanham, MD: Lexington Books, 2016).

134. A luminous account of the defeat of Madison's plan, emphasizing the delegates' practical as opposed to philosophic bent, is John P. Roche, "The Founding Fathers: A Reform Caucus in Action," *American Political Science Review* 55, no. 4 (December 1961): 799, 803–10, https://www.cambridge.org/core/journals/american-political-science-review/article/abs/founding-fathers-a-reform-caucus-in-action/CE50156024A1189BFA965DBBE1094B3A. The recent, now definitive study of the Philadelphia Convention is Klarman, *The Founders' Coup*, 126–304.

135. US Const. art. I, § 10.

136. Ellis, *American Creation*, 117.

137. *Federalist*, no. 10 (Madison).

138. *Federalist*, no. 39 (James Madison).

139. *Federalist*, no. 51 (James Madison).

140. Edward C. Banfield, "Was the Founding an Accident?," in *Here the People Rule: Selected Essays*, 2nd. ed. (Washington, DC: AEI Press, 1991), 7, https://www.aei.org/wp-content/uploads/2014/07/-here-the-people-rule_165254919061.pdf.

141. The contract clause, however, was inserted at the last minute, probably by Hamilton, in words much broader than those of an earlier proposal (directed narrowly at debtor-relief laws) that had been rejected. See McDonald, "The Constitution and Hamiltonian Capitalism," 49, 59–64. An excellent study of the genesis of the intellectual property clause is B. Zorina Khan, "Looking Backward: Founding Choices in Innovation and Intellectual Property Protection," in Irwin and Sylla, *Founding Choices*, 315.

142. Local governments in Britain and the Dutch Republic possessed significant independent authority over trade and other matters at the time of the US founding. See Barry R. Weingast, "The Economic Role of Political Institutions: Market-Preserving Federalism and Economic Development," *Journal of Law, Economics, and Organization* 11, no. 1 (April 1995): 1, https://academic.oup.com/jleo/article-abstract/11/1/814966. But the arrangements were less formal and structured than those of the US Constitution and were not templates for American federalism.

143. The definitive account is Paul Johnson, *The Birth of the Modern: World Society 1815–1830* (New York: HarperCollins, 1991). Alan Greenspan and Adrian Woolridge emphasize the importance of America's entrepreneurial culture to the cascade of inventions and new technologies in the early 1800s in Greenspan and Woolridge, *Capitalism in America*, 40–54.

144. Specialization, like competition, is a fundamental principle of market economics—the first chapter of *The Wealth of Nations* is devoted to explaining the advantages of the division of labor. One might say that "the policy of supplying, by specialization in knowledge and function, the defect of better understanding and ability, might be traced through the whole system of human affairs, private as well as public."

145. The four senator-presidents were Benjamin Harrison, Warren Harding, John F. Kennedy, and Barack Obama. Data through George W. Bush are presented in Christopher DeMuth, "Governors (and Generals) Rule," *American Enterprise* (January–February 2004), https://ccdemuth.com//wp-content/uploads/2015/03/governors_and_genrals_rule.pdf.

146. The ensuing discussion of banking draws on Charles W. Calomiris and Stephen H. Haber, *Fragile by Design: The Political Origins of Banking Crises and Scarce Credit* (Princeton, NJ: Princeton University Press, 2014), 153–202; McCraw, *The Founders and Finance*, 74–121, 227–306; Hammond, *Banks and Politics in America*, 114–285; Rousseau and Sylla, "Emerging Financial Markets and Early U.S. Growth"; Sylla, "Financial Foundations," 59; Rousseau, "Monetary Policy and the Dollar," 121; and Howard Bodenhorn, "Federal and State Commercial Banking in the Federalist Era and Beyond," in Irwin and Sylla, *Founding Choices*, 151.

147. Sylla, "Financial Foundations," 74.

148. Hammond, *Banks and Politics in America*, 124.

149. Calomiris and Haber, *Fragile by Design*, 163.

150. John Joseph Wallis, "The Other Foundings: Federalism and the Constitutional Structure of American Government," in Irwin and Sylla, *Founding Choices*, 177, 183–88.

151. Calomiris and Haber, *Fragile by Design*, 166.

152. Brad Littlejohn, "National Conservatism, Then and Now," *National Affairs* 60 (Summer 2023): 165, https://www.nationalaffairs.com/publications/detail/national-conservatism-then-and-now.

153. Drew R. McCoy, *The Elusive Republic: Political Economy in Jeffersonian America* (Chapel Hill, NC: University of North Carolina Press, 1980), 223–33.

154. Thomas Jefferson, "From Thomas Jefferson to the United States Congress," December 2, 1806, Founders Online, https://founders.archives.gov/documents/Jefferson/99-01-02-4616.

155. McCoy, *The Elusive Republic*, 188.

156. Hammond, *Banks and Politics in America*, 443.

157. Howard Bodenhorn, "Antebellum Banking in the United States," Economic History Association, 2023, https://eh.net/encyclopedia/antebellum-banking-in-the-united-states.

158. Wallis, "The Other Foundings," 194–201.

159. Wallis, "The Other Foundings," 201–10; Calomiris and Haber, *Fragile by Design*, 168–71; Wright, "Rise of the Corporation Nation," 230–33; and Lamoreaux and Wallis, "Economic Crisis, General Laws, and the Mid-Nineteenth-Century Transformation of American Political Economy," 415–18, 423–28, 433.

160. Bodenhorn, "Federal and State Commercial Banking Policy in the Federalist Era and Beyond," 151, 167–69.

161. Howard Bodenhorn, *State Banking in Early America: A New Economic History* (New York: Oxford University Press, 2002).

162. Rousseau and Sylla, "Emerging Financial Markets and Early U.S. Growth," 4.

About the Authors

Jay Cost is the Gerald R. Ford nonresident senior fellow at the American Enterprise Institute, where he focuses on political theory, Congress, and elections. He is also a visiting scholar at Grove City College and a contributing editor at the *Washington Examiner*.

Christopher DeMuth is a distinguished fellow in American thought in the Heritage Foundation's B. Kenneth Simon Center for American Studies.

Richard A. Epstein is the inaugural Laurence A. Tisch Professor of Law at the New York University School of Law, where he serves as a director of the Classical Liberal Institute, which he helped found in 2013. He has served as the Peter and Kirstin Bedford Senior Fellow at the Hoover Institution since 2000.

Clement Fatovic is a professor of politics and international relations at Florida International University.

Deirdre Nansen McCloskey is a distinguished scholar and Isaiah Berlin Chair in Liberal Thought at the Cato Institute and distinguished professor emerita of economics and history and professor emerita of English and communication at the University of Illinois at Chicago.

About the Editors

Yuval Levin is the director of Social, Cultural, and Constitutional Studies at the American Enterprise Institute, where he also holds the Beth and Ravenel Curry Chair in Public Policy. The founder and editor of *National Affairs*, he is also a senior editor at the *New Atlantis*, a contributing editor at *National Review*, and a contributing opinion writer at the *New York Times*.

Adam J. White is a senior fellow at the American Enterprise Institute, where he focuses on the Supreme Court and the administrative state. Concurrently, he codirects the Antonin Scalia Law School's C. Boyden Gray Center for the Study of the Administrative State.

John Yoo is a nonresident senior fellow at the American Enterprise Institute; the Emanuel S. Heller Professor of Law at the University of California, Berkeley; and a visiting fellow at the Hoover Institution.

The American Enterprise Institute for Public Policy Research

AEI is a nonpartisan, nonprofit research and educational organization. The work of our scholars and staff advances ideas rooted in our commitment to expanding individual liberty, increasing opportunity, and strengthening freedom.

The Institute engages in research; publishes books, papers, studies, and short-form commentary; and conducts seminars and conferences. AEI's research activities are carried out under four major departments: Domestic Policy Studies, Economic Policy Studies, Foreign and Defense Policy Studies, and Social, Cultural, and Constitutional Studies. The resident scholars and fellows listed in these pages are part of a network that also includes nonresident scholars at top universities.

The views expressed in AEI publications are those of the authors; AEI does not take institutional positions on any issues.

www.ingramcontent.com/pod-product-compliance
Lightning Source LLC
Jackson TN
JSHW080733070325
80345JS00002B/53